PRIMERS

Performance-Oriented Architecture

PRIMERS

Performance-Oriented Architecture

Rethinking Architectural Design and the Built Environment

MICHAEL HENSEL

A John Wiley and Sons, Ltd, Publication

This edition first published 2013
© 2013 John Wiley & Sons Ltd

Registered office
John Wiley & Sons Ltd, The Atrium, Southern Gate, Chichester, West Sussex, PO19 8SQ,
United Kingdom

For details of our global editorial offices, for customer services and for information about
how to apply for permission to reuse the copyright material in this book please see our
website at www.wiley.com.

Wiley publishes in a variety of print and electronic formats and by print-on-demand. Some
material included with standard print versions of this book may not be included in e-books or
in print-on-demand. If this book refers to media such as a CD or DVD that is not included in
the version you purchased, you may download this material at http://booksupport.wiley.com.
For more information about Wiley products, visit www.wiley.com.

Designations used by companies to distinguish their products are often claimed as
trademarks. All brand names and product names used in this book are trade names, service
marks, trademarks or registered trademarks of their respective owners. The publisher is not
associated with any product or vendor mentioned in this book.

Limit of Liability/Disclaimer of Warranty: while the publisher and author have used their
best efforts in preparing this book, they make no representations or warranties with respect
to the accuracy or completeness of the contents of this book and specifically disclaim
any implied warranties of merchantability or fitness for a particular purpose. It is sold on
the understanding that the publisher is not engaged in rendering professional services
and neither the publisher nor the author shall be liable for damages arising herefrom.
If professional advice or other expert assistance is required, the services of a competent
professional should be sought.

ISBN 978-0-470-97332-5 (hardback)
ISBN 978-0-470-97331-8 (paperback)
ISBN 978-1-118-57011-1 (ebk)
ISBN 978-1-118-57012-8 (ebk)
ISBN 978-1-118-57013-5 (ebk)
ISBN 978-1-118-64063-0 (ebk)

Executive Commissioning Editor: Helen Castle
Project Editor: Miriam Swift
Assistant Editor: Calver Lezama

Cover design, page design and layouts by Karen Willcox, www.aleatoria.com
Front cover image © Michael Hensel. With thanks to:
Julia King and Louis Gadd (layer 1); Dae Song Lee (layer 2).
Printed in Italy by Printer Trento Srl

Dedication

To my wife, mother and late father with much love.

Acknowledgements

This *AD Primer* offers a theoretical framework for an inclusive approach to architecture, the built environment and questions of sustainability. It stems from what continues to be an invigorating and prolific collaboration with much-valued friends and colleagues, researchers and students to whom I am profoundly grateful.

I wish to express my heartfelt appreciation to my numerous companions and collaborators en route to *performance-oriented architecture.* To name but a few, I offer thanks to my long-term companions at the OCEAN Design Research Association and at the Sustainable Environment Association (SEA), and in particular my friends and colleagues Ludo Grooteman, Prof Dr Christopher Hight, Dr Pavel Hladik, Prof Dr David Jolly Monge, Sabine Kraft, Prof Dr David Leatherbarrow, Prof Dr Birger Sevaldson, Jeffrey Turko and Prof Dr Julian Vincent for their generous support. As the core of this work was developed in my PhD thesis I wish to express my sincerest gratitude to my supervisor Prof Emeritus Dr George Jeronimidis, as well as to the University of Reading for bestowing a DTA grant, which made it possible for me to undertake my PhD. My sincere gratitude belongs also to my committed students at the Oslo School of Architecture and Design, the Architectural Association, the Izmir University of Economics, the Rice School of Architecture, the University of Technology in Sydney, and numerous other schools, who have tremendously contributed to this work through their dedicated individual and collective efforts.

My deepest gratitude belongs to my wife Defne Sunguroğlu Hensel for her continuous contributions, constructive criticism, invigorating enthusiasm and steadfast support and patience, and to my mother and late father who made absolutely everything possible for me.

For many years of highly committed and constructive collaboration on numerous publications, and this book in particular, I am most grateful to Helen Castle, commissioning editor of *AD* at John Wiley & Sons. Many thanks also to Miriam Swift, Calver Lezama, Abigail Grater and Karen Willcox for their committed work on this book.

This *Primer* can obviously only provide a brief introduction to a complex subject that keeps evolving and that requires a much more extensive and sustained discussion. I take full responsibility for any shortcomings that may result from its necessary conciseness.

Contents

Foreword

This book's ambition is considerable. A different style of thinking is called for, one that rejects long-standing habits of thought in favour of a focus on *performance*. The theme is not presented as new to architecture, just newly significant, because the object-oriented methods that still dominate design and criticism have brought the field to a critical condition. I suspect that the ideas and projects set forth in this text will attract wide readership; but like many topics that garner popular interest this one is understood in many ways. The real force of this book's thesis can only be grasped if its sense of performance is distinguished from usage that merely renames old conceptions.

Many designers and critics regard architecture as a particular form of representation. The common idea is that the buildings that have been designed creatively are meant to be perceived aesthetically and valued economically, in the interrelated transactions of experience and exchange. An innovative opera house, for example, brings pleasure to its spectators, fame to its designer, and revenue to its owner, or home city. Assumptions about the visual character of architectural experience support this view, as do ideas of design authorship. Although current, this way of understanding and describing buildings adopts premises that were proposed centuries ago and then subsequently naturalised in professional writings and public discussion, which is why we take it for granted uncritically. More importantly, this conception ignores the fact that the full sense of a built work is neither immediate nor transparent, despite recent accounts of design as a form of branding, and associated ideas of the work as a cultural commodity. A distant view merely initiates a sequence of perceptions – some visual, some tactile or motor, and others auditory – that successively augment and qualify the initial perception. Nor is a building's role in practical affairs limited to signification. This is because buildings are at once representational and *operational*. When the architectural image is tied to the building's modes of performance, when the work's look is linked to its behaviours, its ways of responding to environmental forces and the requirements of inhabitation, the inadequacy of the idea of the building as something designed for an appreciative glance becomes obvious. This *Primer* advances this more complete vision: *the building reveals what it does*.

The *performative turn* in other fields – theatre and linguistics especially – parallels and may have prompted the growing concern for *performance* in architecture. Perhaps the first question to be asked of current ideas is whether or not they advance anything more than old-style (early-modern) functionalism; which is to say, the long-familiar idea that utility is the essence of the architectural solution, that buildings are really instruments in service of some clearly specified purpose, that form – after all – is the result of function. Perhaps all that has changed in recent years is technique, now that instruments of measuring and modelling give us outcomes that are more certain and objectively descriptive. What, if anything, is really new in current thinking about performance, in this *Primer* in particular?

The idea that well-defined functions or space-specific uses are decisive in architecture has appealed to many over the past several decades because it is entirely congenial to the technical nature of modern design practice. In both functional and technical thinking, foresight is key. It is the business of design to anticipate and govern both construction and occupation. Buildings themselves are likewise anticipatory, for when they are designed to serve specific needs they anticipate practical affairs. Architecture is thus doubly preparatory. So much for the functionalist stance.

This position will be overcome only when the preparations of a well-designed construction are seen to be inevitably inadequate, when the finished work is understood to be necessarily incomplete, because the world of which it is part is recognised as a field of forces that will, over time and unpredictably, re-qualify what design and construction had pre-qualified. Engagement with what will change redefines the work. The building's interactions with changing conditions of use and the environment – necessary interactions, if the work is to fulfil its purposes – mean that it eventually becomes something other than what design intended. When the building is understood as the locus of performances (not functional solutions), it can be seen as both a preparation and a response; an ensemble of conditions that not only anticipates occurrences but reacts to them, by virtue of foresight in the first case and participation in the second. The idea of participation (involvement, or 'embeddedness' in the arguments of the text that follows) suggests a simple ratio: what a part is to its counterpart, the work is to the world. And once our plans for the work allow it to act in concert with the play of social and natural forces, its harmonies will enrich our lives in ways that are at once unexpected and wonderful.

David Leatherbarrow

'The environment must be organised so that its own regeneration and reconstruction does not constantly disrupt its performance.'

Christopher Alexander, *Notes on the Synthesis of Form*, Harvard University Press (Cambridge, MA), 1964, p 3

'The notion of environment (*milieu*) is becoming a universal and required way of capturing both the experience and the existence of living beings and we could almost speak of it being a category of contemporary thought.'

Georges Canguilhem, 'Le vivant et son milieu' [1952], *La Connaissance de la vie*, J Vrin (Paris), 1980, p 129 (translation by Graham Burchell)

'Above all we must remember that nothing that exists or comes into being, lasts or passes, can be thought of as entirely isolated, entirely unadulterated. One thing is always permeated, accompanied, covered, or enveloped by another; it produces effects and endures them. And when so many things work through one another, where are we to find the insight and discover what governs and what serves, what leads the way and what follows?'

Johann Wolfgang von Goethe, 'Versuch einer Witterungslehre' (1825), translation in D Miller, *Goethe: Scientific Studies*, Suhrkamp (New York), 1988, pp 145–6

'One can start from the idea that the world is filled not, in the first instance, with facts and observations, but with agency. The world, I want to say, is continually doing things, things that bear upon us … as forces upon material beings.'

Andrew Pickering, *The Mangle of Practice: Time, Agency and Science*, University of Chicago Press (Chicago, IL), 1995, p 6

Introduction
The Task
at Hand

Architects continually tackle the question as to what architectures should be and do, why this should be so, and how desired results could be accomplished. Much less frequently a considerably more significant question is asked, upon which the answer to the previous questions hinges: what is architecture, what are its core knowledge fields and what are its tasks?

Perhaps the answer to this question may seem too obvious for most to engage with seriously. After all, architectural handbooks, contracts, curricula and syllabi seem to deliver clear enough descriptions of the content matter of architectural practice and education. By combining these with the widespread supposition that architecture is a generalist profession which straddles the intersection between the arts, humanities and science, one could surely devise a sufficiently detailed universal statement about the discipline. And yet, this approach seems unsatisfactory for several reasons. For one, it would seem that handbooks, contracts, curricula and syllabi must be formulated according to a rather specific definition of the discipline in order to be instrumental. Secondly, it would seem of fundamental importance to recognise that the discipline evolves and changes together with the kind, range and complexity of its time-specific contexts and tasks. This has a significant impact not only on the definition of the perpetually shifting knowledge fields of architecture, but also on the consideration as to the other disciplines (such as engineering) with which it should seek affiliation. Therefore, if an attempt to define what architecture and its tasks are is based on the recognition of its inherently time- and task-specific characteristic, it becomes obvious that any such approach has a finite applicability. Configuring an approach that is open and inclusive enough to be adjusted, while at the same time being adequately integrated, may extend this duration.

As it would seem, architectural discourse has over recent decades become both increasingly diverse and fragmented. The beginning of this development cannot be assigned to any singular event or time. Numerous social, cultural and economic factors may have played their role in it throughout the previous century. At present, despite certain recurring themes, no discernible dominant architectural discourse appears to exist. This could be seen as an indication that the discipline has matured to the point where alternative choices are at hand when needed. However, today the field is dominated by specialist discourses that focus on more isolated topics. It may be argued that this development mirrors what is taking place in other disciplines where specialisation is accelerated to such an extent that general overviews are becoming increasingly difficult due to the amount of research and dissemination in each specialist field. With this in mind, it seems clear that architecture is urgently in need of integrative approaches that begin to coalesce specialist discourses for the sake of encouraging concerted efforts towards improving upon the built environment and its debilitating impact on the natural environment.

The task of this *AD Primer* is to provide a suitable framework for a specific definition of architecture and a cohesive discourse. It offers an integrated approach to architectural design, the built environment and questions of sustainability, entitled *performance-oriented architecture*, and examines relevant core concepts and specific traits in search of an architecture that is in the service of the natural environment. This has necessitated drawing on a number of disciplines. Emphasis is placed on the spatial and material organisation of architecture and its interaction with the environment. The aim is to arrive at an approach that is relevant to everyday architecture.

1

A Brief History
of the Notion of
Performance

The notion of performance emerged in the humanities and social sciences in the mid-20th century and, following this development, also in the arts and science in general. It took shape during the 1940s and 1950s with an intellectual movement known as the *performative turn*: a paradigm shift in the humanities and social sciences, with a focus on theorising *performance* as a social and cultural element. Key to the movement were the works of Kenneth Duva Burke, Victor Witter Turner, Erving Goffman and others, which focused on the elaboration of a dramaturgical paradigm to be applied to culture at large and that facilitated the view of all culture as performance.[1] Similarly influential were the writings of the British philosopher of language John L Austin, who posited that speech constitutes an *active* practice that can affect and transform realities.[2] Due to the movement, performance is today commonly understood as a concept that provides a path to understanding human behaviour. This is rooted in the hypothesis that all human practices are performed and are affected by their specific context: the notion of *active human agency*.

The performative turn movement inspired a similar development in the arts. Fine art, music, literature and theatre all – in the words of Erika Fischer-Lichte, Professor of Theatre Studies at the Freie Universität Berlin – 'tend to realise themselves through *acts* (performances)', thus shifting the emphasis from *works* to *events* that increasingly involve the 'recipients, listeners, spectators'.[3] Furthermore, Fischer-Lichte proposed that Austin's notion of the performative is not only applicable to speech, but that it can also be applied to corporeal acts. This relates to the development of the 'performance arts' as situation-specific, action-emphasising and ephemeral artistic presentations of a performer. It thus engages spatial and temporal aspects, as well as the performer and a specific relation between performer and audience.

Subsequently the concept of performance also began to surface in the natural sciences, technology studies and economic science. Andrew Pickering, Professor of Sociology and Philosophy at the University of Exeter, charted a shift within the sciences away from a 'representational idiom' and towards a 'performative' one, proposing that:

> Within an expanded conception of scientific culture ... – one that goes beyond science-as-knowledge, to include material, social and temporal dimensions of science – it becomes possible to imagine that science is not just about representation ... One can start from the idea that the world is filled not, in the first instance, with facts and observations, but with agency. The world, I want to say, is continually doing things, things that bear upon us not as observation statements upon disembodied intellects but as forces upon material beings.[4]

Pickering went on to write that 'practice effects associations between multiple and often heterogeneous cultural elements', as well as operates the production of knowledge and scientific activity as a way of *doing things*.[5] In so doing, Pickering paved the way for an understanding of active human agency in the context of the sciences, and of the world being filled with and intrinsically characterised by active agency.

It becomes necessary at this point to clarify the concept of *agency*. In philosophy and sociology, agency refers to the capacity of a person or entity to act in the world. While studies of human agency are generally characterised by differences in understanding within and between disciplines, it is not usually contested as a general concept. The concept of *non-human agency*, however, has remained to some extent controversial. *Actor–network theory* as developed by Michel Callon, Bruno Latour, John Law and others is a social theory that postulates non-human agency as one of its core features. Bruno Latour explained that:

> If action is limited a priori to what 'intentional', 'meaningful' humans do, it is hard to see how a hammer, a basket, a door closer, a cat, a rug, a mug, a

list, or a tag could act. They might exist in the domain of 'material' 'causal' relations, but not in the 'reflexive' 'symbolic' domain of social relations. By contrast, if we stick to our decision to start from the controversies about actors and agencies, then *any thing* that does modify a state of affairs by making a difference is an actor – or, if it has no figuration yet, an actant. Thus, the questions to ask about any agent are simply the following: Does it make a difference in the course of some other agent's action or not? Is there some trial that allows someone to detect this difference?[6]

Latour referred to such items as '*participants* in the course of action awaiting to be given figuration'.[7] Moreover, Latour argued that such participants can operate on the entire range from determining to serving human actions and from full causality to none, and called for analysis 'to account for the durability and extension of any interaction'.[8] The proposed grading of causality is of interest in that it can serve as a systematic approach to specific aspects of performance-oriented architecture.

There are several fundamental criticisms of actor–network theory. One key criticism focuses on the property of *intentionality* as a fundamental distinction between humans and animals or objects. Activity theory, for instance, operates on intentionality as a fundamental requirement and thus ascribes agency exclusively to humans. In contrast, the concept of agency in actor–network theory is not based on intentionality, and nor does it assign intentionality to non-human agents.

Recognising non-human agency does not, however, necessitate the relinquishing of concerns for human intentionality. If architecture is thought to perform, this requires some concept of non-human agency and the integration of different forms and lack of intentionality in agency.

Moreover, the notion of agency is based on that of *environment* – a term which itself has greatly varying definitions and implications and therefore requires clarification. Thomas Brandstetter and Karin Harrasser highlighted two works that were key to the development of the related notions of *ambiance* and *milieu* from the 1940s onwards: Leo Spitzer's 'Milieu and Ambience: An Essay in Historical Semantics' of 1942, and Georges Canguilhem's lecture from 1946–7 later published under the title 'Le vivant et son milieu'.[9] Spitzer traced the development of the concept of ambiance from the Greek *periechon* and Latin *ambiens*, via the notion of medium, to the modern notions of ambiance and milieu. Canguilhem started from the 18th-century import of the notion of environment from mechanics into biology. Both cite Isaac Newton (1642–1727), who used the notion of *medium* to refer to ether as the locus of gravitational force, and Auguste Comte (1798–1857), who extended the French term *milieu* to encompass not only the physical medium that surrounds an organism, but also the general scope of external conditions that are necessary to support the organism's existence. Where they differ, according to Brandstetter and Harrasser, is in assessing the work of the biologist Jakob von Uexküll (1864–1944) who examined how living beings perceive their environment subjectively. Von Uexküll posited that:

> All reality is subjective appearance. …
> Kant set the subject, man, over against objects, and discovered the fundamental principles according to which objects are built up by our minds.
> …
> The task of biology consists in expanding in two directions the results of Kant's investigations:
> (i) by considering the part played by our body, and especially by our sense-organs and central nervous system, and
> (ii) by studying the relations of other subjects (animals) to objects.[10]

Von Uexküll introduced a distinction between the general surrounding (*Umgebung*) and subjectively perceived environments (*Umwelt*), and between the latter and the inner world (*Innenwelt*) of an organism. The study of the relation of animals to their environments or *Umwelten* led Von Uexküll to argue that all organisms are subjects, because they react to perceived sensory data as signs. This gave rise to a field of study in biology entitled *biosemiotics*, a termed coined by the psychiatrist and semiotician Friedrich Rothschild (1899–1995). As Kalevi Kull explained:

> Biology has studied how organisms and living communities are built. But it is no less important to understand what such living systems know, in a broad sense; that is, what they remember (what agent-object sign relations are biologically preserved), what they recognize (what distinction they are capable and not capable of), what signs they explore (how they communicate, make meaning and use signs) and so on. These questions are all about how different living systems perceive the world, what experience motivates what actions, based on those perceptions.[11]

This notion of the subjective perception of *Umwelt* offers an interesting approach to the notion of environment in that it involves the organism's active agency and relates to the approach of agency in actor–network theory. As Brandstetter and Harrasser pointed out, Spitzer was critical in his 1942 article of a pronounced leaning to determinism in relation to specific scientific notions of milieu and *Umwelt*.[12] In contrast, Canguilhem argued that Von Uexküll's notion of *Umwelt* took adequate account of the 'irreducible activity of life'.[13] He maintained that:

> man's specific environment is not situated in the universal environment like content in its container. ... A living being is not reducible to a meeting point of influences. Whence the inadequacy of any biology which, through complete submission to the spirit of the physicochemical sciences, would eliminate from its domain every consideration of meaning. A meaning, from the biological and psychological point of view, is an assessment of values in keeping with a need.[14]

Whether one concurs with Canguilhem's assessment of need or not, it seems clear that, when considering agency of different species, their perception of their specific environment is key.

Thus the discipline of biosemiotics can provide an insightful approach to questions of agency of different species, and can perhaps offer an inroad to rethinking concerns of meaning that are present in post-modern approaches to questions of performance in architecture. At any rate, biosemiotics and architecture are not yet affiliated disciplines and research needs to commence in this intersection of knowledge fields.

References

1 See, for example: K Burke, *Language as Symbolic Action*, University of California Press (Berkeley, CA; Los Angeles, CA), 1966; VW Turner, *The Forest of Symbols: Aspects of Ndembu Ritual*, Cornell University Press (Ithaca, NY), 1967; VW Turner, *Dramas, Fields and Metaphors: Symbolic Action in Human Society*, Cornell University Press (Ithaca, NY), 1974; E Goffman, *The Presentation of Self in Everyday Life*, Anchor Books (New York), 1959; E Goffman, *Where the Action Is*, Allen Lane (London), 1969.

2 JL Austin, *How to Do Things with Words*, Clarendon Press (Oxford), 1962.

3 E Fischer-Lichte, *Ästhetik des Performativen*, Suhrkamp (Frankfurt), 2004, p 29.

4 A Pickering, *The Mangle of Practice: Time, Agency and Science*, University of Chicago Press (Chicago, IL), 1995, pp 5–6.

5 Ibid, p 95.

6 B Latour, *Reassembling the Social: An Introduction to Actor-Network-Theory*, Oxford University Press (Oxford), 2005, p 71.

7 Ibid.

8 Ibid, p 72.

9 T Brandstetter and K Harrasser, 'Introduction', in T Brandstetter, K Harrasser and G Friesinger (eds), *Das Leben und seine Räume*, Turia + Kant (Vienna), 2010, pp 9–20; L Spitzer, 'Milieu and Ambience: An Essay in Historical Semantics', *Philosophy and Phenomenological Research*, Vol 3, 1942, pp 1–42, 169–218; G Canguilhem, 'Le vivant et son milieu' [1952], *La connaissance de la vie*, J Vrin (Paris), 1980, pp 129–54.

10 J von Uexküll, *Umwelt und Innenwelt der Tiere*, Julius Springer (Berlin), 1909, p xv.

11 L Else, 'A Meadowful of Meaning', *New Scientist*, 21 August 2010, Vol 207, No 2774, pp 28–31 (p 31).

12 Brandstetter and Harrasser, 'Introduction', in T Brandstetter, K Harrasser and G Friesinger (eds), *Das Leben und seine Räume*, op cit, p 14.

13 Ibid, p 16.

14 Canguilhem, 'Le vivant et son milieu', op cit (translation by Graham Burchell).

2

A Brief History of the Notion of Performance in Architecture

In the context of the wide range of architectural discourses today, the notion of *performance* is a particularly prominent and enduring one. A number of historical factors have had a key role in its emergence. These arguably began with the impact of scientific developments on architecture, in particular biology, from the mid-18th century onwards. Then followed the rise of the notions of *environment*, *milieu* and *Umwelt* in the writings of Auguste Comte, Jakob von Uexküll and others (see chapter 1). In the 20th century, architecture took on board systems theory,[1] and the cross-disciplinary *performative turn* movement (see chapter 1) had a significant impact. More recent years have seen the further development of critical discourse in architecture coupled with increasing efforts in research by design.

The 1960s witnessed one of the most complex systems-engineering projects ever: the United States' National Aeronautics and Space Administration's (NASA) Apollo human space-flight programme (1961–72). The space race and the Cold War-related construction of nuclear shelter bunkers necessitated the design of contained life- or 'eco'-systems that required a far more complex approach to design and engineering than ever before. In this context, in August 1967 the US-American journal *Progressive Architecture* (*PA*) dedicated an entire issue to a topic of performance, entitled *Performance Design*. As points of origin for this architectural approach, *PA* listed *systems analysis*, *systems engineering* and *operations research* – all essentially oriented towards hard systems. Emphasis was therefore placed on methods of addressing complex engineering problems, which involved mathematical modelling towards optimisation and efficiency. While concerns with balancing quantitative and qualitative measures were voiced, and certain unquantifiable issues such as aesthetics were recognised and discussed, the shortcoming of *PA*'s portrayal of the subject was its almost exclusive alignment with the hard-systems approach. This required that design problems be fully described a priori, so that the focus was on problem solving through methods that are not equipped to account for unquantifiable variables, dealing instead mainly with questions of *efficiency*, *effectiveness* and *optimisation*. In some ways this was a self-defeating process, as the number of progressively tighter standards that arose from the emphasis on efficiency and optimisation gradually replaced the systems approach in architecture and a number of other disciplines.

At the same time, in the late 1960s, the critique of Functionalism and hard-systems approaches in architecture drew the rudder in a number of different directions. Functionalism and Rationalism became the foci of architectural debates and triggered in their wake numerous counter-reactions: Neo-Functionalism, Neo-Rationalism, Post-Functionalism etc. From here two notable parallel reactions began to take shape. One was a succinct critique of programme as a deterministic approach to the relation between space and space use, rooted in hard-systems approaches. The other was based on the gradual rise of semiotics in architecture and triggered the movement towards locating performance in the meaning of architecture, the symbolic. The latter approach fostered the ascent of Post-Modernism in architecture, which was in turn criticised from the late 1980s onwards as operating on a limited set of culturally determined references and thus finite repertoire incapable of producing a new architecture. The emphasis shifted instead to more abstract formal experimentation and the restatement of criteria for a new architecture, as well as the production of *architectural effects*.[2]

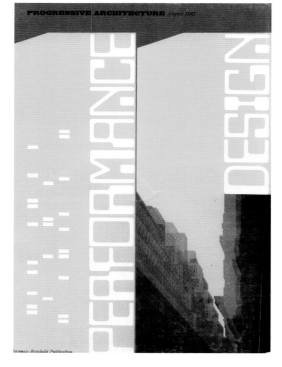

Progressive Architecture, August 1967
Cover of the issue of the journal *Progressive Architecture* that focused on Performance Design.

The past decade has witnessed a gradual return of an explicit interest in the relation between architecture and performance. At this present juncture there seem to be perhaps five different approaches towards performance in architecture.

The first of these approaches emerged from an interest in representation, symbolism and meaning in architecture from the late 1960s onwards through the efforts of Charles Jencks and others.[3] Jencks posited that 'Radical Eclecticism is multivalent, as against so much Modern architecture: it pulls together different kinds of meaning, which appeal to opposite faculties of the mind and the body, so that they interrelate and modify each other.'[4] Jencks's pursuit of Post-Modernism in architecture swiftly attracted broad criticism in the wake of a diversifying critical discourse. Kenneth Frampton argued that 'the arts have … continued to gravitate, if not towards entertainment, then certainly towards commodity and – in the case of that which Charles Jencks has since classified as Post-Modern architecture – towards pure technique and scenography'.[5] Moreover, Andreas Huyssen warned that 'postmodernist avant-garde … is not only the end game of avant-gardism. It also represents the fragmentation and decline of critical adversary culture.'[6] Jeffrey Kipnis pursued a two-pronged criticism, positing that 'Post-modernism's critique of the politics of erasure / replacement and emphasis on recombination have also led to its greatest abuse, for it has enabled a reactionary discourse that re-establishes traditional hierarchies and supports received systems of power', and that:

> post-modern collage is an extensive practice wholly dependent on effecting incoherent contradictions within and against a dominant frame. As it becomes the prevailing institutional practice, it loses both its contradictory force and its affirmative incoherence. Rather than destabilising an existing context, it operates more and more to inscribe its own institutional space. The only form collage produces, therefore, is the form of collage.[7]

In the wake of the re-emerging interest in performance in architecture, Charles Jencks's approach resurfaced and gained a second lease of life portrayed by an issue of the *AD* journal entitled *Radical Post-Modernism*, reissuing Jencks's predilection both for the 'radical' and for 'Post-Modernism'.[8] In the introduction to the issue Jencks put forward three core concepts that underpin the notion of 'Radical Post-Modernism'. He defined these as follows:

Communication, and its attendant qualities – metaphor, iconography, symbolism, image, surface, narrative, irony – was one value that ties together the 1960s concerns and those of today. ... *formal tropes* of today's Post-Modernism obviously grew out of yesterday: complexity and contradiction, ornament and multiple articulation, collage and juxtaposition, layering and ambiguity, multivalence and double coding. ... *Social content* is the third concern that underlies our common definition of radical, framed in several ways.[9]

This rehashed approach to Post-Modernism appears, however, not to have taken on the scope of criticism that had arisen since its first incarnation. Instead the argument presented in *Radical Post-Modernism* seems to focus on detecting or showcasing the stated features of Post-Modernist architecture in a broad range of projects (some of which were ironically designed by architects who joined the vanguard of critique of Post-Modernist collage in the 1990s) so as to derive a claim of sustained relevance. Moreover, 'radical eclecticism' is upon architecture once again, driven by the divorce of form from structure, envelope from interior, and so on. Sylvia Lavin, for instance, proposed the notion of the 'free skin' that is 'free from formal and expressive obligations to the interior and is free to develop its own qualities and performance criteria'.[10] This position embraces eclecticism by way of contrasting the different elements that constitute a given architecture and thus continues forcefully the predisposition that favours division over integration. Ultimately Lavin's call for 'techniques of cunning, scenography, special effects, theatre and energy' brings this approach full circle back to Frampton's critique of Post-Modernist architects' exclusive focus on technique and scenography.[11]

The second and third approaches to the notion of performance in architecture originate largely from the deep-seated debate over the relationship between form and function that has been dominant in its various guises in architectural discourse since the 1930s. The related approaches to performance can thus chiefly be divided into the formal and the functional, and frequently coincide with the related art–science dialectic in architecture. Thus the formal approach tends to focus on the 'artistic' aspect, while the functional emphasis is frequently associated with science and, more specifically, engineering. Both camps of the form/function and art/engineering divide often foreground either object, subject, environment, atmosphere or event, and sometimes combinations thereof, with the former criticising the latter for being too rigid and the latter criticising the former for

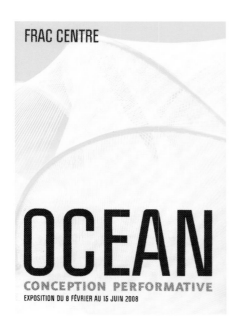

FRAC CENTRE

OCEAN

CONCEPTION PERFORMATIVE
EXPOSITION DU 8 FÉVRIER AU 15 JUIN 2008

*OCEAN: Conception
Performative*
exhibition catalogue,
2008
Cover of the catalogue
to the OCEAN exhibition
'Conception Performative'
at FRAC – Le Fonds régional
d'art contemporain in
Orléans.

being too elusive. Numerous publications on performance in architecture since the late 1960s give ample evidence of this prevailing predisposition.[12]

In their emphasis on division, eclecticism and exclusively formal or functional takes on performance, these three approaches constitute antitheses to an integrated approach to performance.

The fourth approach foregrounds the notion of *event*. This counters any planned relation between architectures and their uses, and emphasises unplanned appropriations and inadvertent latent capacities of architectures. Commenting on the form–function dialectic, Bernard Tschumi argued the importance of the relation between architecture and event:

> There is no architecture without program, without action, without event. … architecture is never autonomous, never pure form, and, similarly, … architecture is not a matter of style and cannot be reduced to a language … [the aim is] to reinstate the term function and, more particularly, to re-inscribe the movement of bodies in space, together with the actions and events that take place within the social and political realm of architecture [and to] refuse the simplistic relation by which form follows function, or use, or socioeconomics.[13]

From a different perspective, Antoine Picon discussed 'the capacity of architecture to become an event, to participate in a world which is more and more often defined in terms of occurrences rather than as a collection of objects and relations'.[14] He continued:

> In a penetrating essay published a few years ago, the philosopher Paul Virilio rightly evokes the growing domination of 'what happens'.[15] As a performing art, or to be more accurate, an art the productions of which are now supposed to perform at various levels, from an ecological footprint to the realm of affects, architecture has become a component of this domination.[16]

The event-related take on performance appears frequently as part of some of the other approaches to performance in architecture. It is often hijacked to sustain arguments which, for the most part, reinstate the form–function dialectic and seek to sustain exclusively formalistic and/or effect-related stances, as well as, in many cases, some form of scenographic neo-eclecticism that by its very nature denies agendas of integration as it operates on distinct differences. It is, however, one key element that performance-oriented architecture needs to address and integrate.

The fifth approach has its origin in a series of efforts that commenced at the beginning of the 21st century. One was initiated by David Leatherbarrow as a series of critiques of prevailing approaches to performance in architecture, focusing on the relation between planned and unplanned performances, between performance, place and purpose, and between a building and its larger context or 'topography'.[17] Leatherbarrow argued that 'a physicalistic understanding of architecture … is inadequate to a building's requirement with respect to human praxis … and misconceived if taken to be wholly adequate to the architectural task'.[18] Moreover he argued 'against the various ways of conceiving the building as self-sustained and internally defined product of design', while also pointing out that 'the city (the concrete embodiment of common culture) is not something that single designs can form, shape, construct, or achieve – only condition and approximate'.[19] Leatherbarrow's approach is both striking and unique in the way it seeks to carefully straddle the complexities which arise from planned and unplanned conditions that architectures encounter, participate in, seek to provide and are modified by across different scales. This approach makes clear that disassociation of these complex relations is inadequate and, instead, they must all be considered as part and parcel of performance in architecture. It thus delivers an erudite outline for an integrated approach.

Other aspects of the currently emerging fifth approach can be discerned in various commentaries from the first few years of the 21st century. Branko Kolarevic and Ali Malkawi, for instance, posited that the 'emphasis on building performance … is influencing building design, its processes and practices, by blurring the distinction between geometry and analysis, between appearance and performance'.[20] In this context David Leatherbarrow charted two different characteristics of performance in architecture which in his view are inseparable:

> the kind that can be exact and unfailing in its predictions of outcomes, and the kind that anticipates what is likely, given the circumstantial contingencies of built work. The first sort is technical and productive, the second

contextual and projective. There is no need to rank these two in a theory of architectural performance; important instead is grasping their reciprocity and joint necessity.[21]

An integrated approach to performance also requires reconsideration of the scope and definition of relevant first principles upon which such an approach relies. Chris Luebkeman, for instance, argued that:

Performance-based design is really about going back to basics and to first principles, taking into account the experience one has gained over time as well as field and laboratory observations about the non-linear behaviour of elements and components. It is the combination of first principles with experience and observations that is the fundamental potential of the design philosophy. It places the design imperative back in the hands of the designer. And, more importantly, it also places responsibility and accountability back into the designer's hands in a very obvious way. One can no longer hide behind building codes.[22]

Given these realisations, the question arises as to why the fifth approach has thus far not come to full fruition. The answer seems clear: performance-oriented architecture requires an overarching and inclusive theoretical framework together with integrated and instrumental concepts, design strategies and methods. It is from this realisation that the objective of this *Primer* – to formulate a basis for an integrative approach towards a performance-oriented architecture – developed. The intention was to strike a balance between providing a tangible theoretical framework and useful concepts that are adaptable according to context and circumstances so as to be useful for everyday practice. This aim resonates with Martin Bechthold's marked insight:

Despite its muddled attitude towards performance it is crucial to move performance-thinking back to the core of the disciplinary consciousness. What could be more timely … at the age of a globally warming planet and dwindling natural resources? … performance-based design should be here to stay, less as an 'ism', but as an ethical obligation to the profession and to society.[23]

When extending the inquiry into performance-oriented architecture to include questions of sustainability, a further question arises: is the perceived diametrical opposition between the man-made and the natural of continued use?

Might it instead be hypothesised that architecture could be *in the service of the natural environment* by way of its inherent agency and its interaction with it? And might this lead to a different thinking about architectural design and provisions made by architectures?

References

1 For systems theory, see: L von Bertalanffy, *General System Theory: Foundations, Development, Applications* [1968], George Braziller (New York), revised edition, 1976.
2 See, for example: RM Unger, 'The Better Futures of Architecture', *Anyone*, Rizzoli (New York), 1991, pp 28–36; J Kipnis, 'Towards a New Architecture', in G Lynn (ed), *Folding in Architecture – AD*, Vol 63, No 3–4, 1993, pp 40–9.
3 See, for example: C Jencks and G Baird (eds), *Meaning in Architecture*, Barrie & Rockliff, The Cresset Press (London), 1969; C Jencks, *The Language of Post-Modern Architecture*, Academy Editions (London), 1977.
4 C Jencks, *The Language of Post-Modern Architecture* [1977], revised edition, Academy Editions (London), 1978, p 132.
5 K Frampton, 'Towards a Critical Regionalism: Six Points for an Architecture of Resistance', in H Foster (ed), *The Anti-Aesthetic: Essays on Postmodern Culture*, Bay Press (Port Townsend, WA), 1983, pp 16–30 (p 19).
6 A Huyssen, 'The Search for Tradition: Avant-Garde and Postmodernism in the 1970s', *New German Critique*, No 22, 1981, pp 23–40.

7 J Kipnis, 'Towards a New Architecture', op cit, p 42.
8 C Jencks and FAT (eds), *Radical Post-Modernism – AD*, Vol 81, No 5, 2011.
9 C Jencks, 'What is Radical Post-Modernism?', in ibid, pp 14–17 (p 15).
10 S Lavin, 'Performing the Contemporary, or: Towards an Even Newer Architecture', in Y Grobman and E Neuman (eds), *Performalism: Form and Performance in Digital Architecture*, Routledge (London), 2012, pp 21–6 (p 25).
11 Ibid, p 21.
12 See, for example: *Progressive Architecture, Performance Design* issue, August 1967; B Kolarevic and A Malkawi, *Performative Architecture: Beyond Instrumentality*, Spon (New York), 2005; Y Grobman and E Neuman (eds), *Performalism: Form and Performance in Digital Architecture – Exhibition Catalogue*, Tel Aviv Museum of Art (Tel Aviv), 2008; Y Grobman and E Neuman (eds), *Performalism: Form and Performance in Digital Architecture*, Routledge (London), 2012.
13 B Tschumi, *Architecture and Disjunction*, MIT Press (Cambridge, MA), 1994, pp 3–4.
14 A Picon, 'Architecture

as Performative Art', in Y Grobman and E Neuman (eds), *Performalism: Form and Performance in Digital Architecture*, Routledge (London), 2012, pp 15–19 (p 18).
15 P Virilio, *Unknown Quantity*, Thames & Hudson (London) and Fondation Cartier pour l'art contemporain (Paris), 2002.
16 Picon, 'Architecture as Performative Art', op cit, p 18.
17 D Leatherbarrow, *Architecture Oriented Otherwise*, Princeton Architectural Press (New York), 2009.
18 Ibid, pp 14–15.
19 Ibid, p 15.
20 Kolarevic and Malkawi, op cit, p 3.
21 Leatherbarrow, *Architecture Oriented Otherwise*, op cit, p 18.
22 C Luebkeman, 'Performance-Based Design', in B Kolarevic (ed), *Architecture in the Digital Age: Design and Manufacturing*, Spon Press (New York; London), 2003, pp 275–88 (pp 284–5).
23 M Bechthold, 'Performalism or Performance-Based Design?', in Y Grobman and E Neuman (eds), *Performalism: Form and Performance in Digital Architecture*, Routledge (London), 2012, pp 49–52 (p 52).

3

Non-Discrete Architectures

Performance-oriented architecture is based on the understanding that architectures unfold their *performative capacity* by being *embedded* in nested orders of complexity and *auxiliary* to numerous conditions and processes: such architectures are essentially *non-discrete*. This approach resonates with Christopher Alexander's statement that 'we ought always really to design with a number of nested, overlapped form-context boundaries in mind'.[1]

Following this premise requires a corresponding reconceptualisation of the relation between architectures and the environments they are set within on a spatial, material and temporal level, considering context- and time-specific exterior-to-interior relations, the associated question of extended threshold conditions and the interaction with a dynamic environment.

However, the majority of today's designs develop in the exact opposite direction: architectures are almost invariably perceived and designed as *discrete* objects. *Discreteness* implies various kinds and degrees of disconnection from a given context in order to stand out and arises from a number of predilections of architectural practice, some of which are related to idiosyncratic or so-called *signature* architectures and the *spectacular*, while others arise from more general trends in practice and the industries involved in the making of the built environment. Therefore it might seem that the notion of *non-discreteness* is antithetical to architectural design for as long as it is primarily the *objectness* of architectures that is of central importance to architects and clients alike. This tendency is further enhanced by the emphasis placed on idiosyncratic expression in highly design-oriented contemporary architecture, which results in objects that celebrate discreteness as their core feature. In such cases the emphasis has in recent years almost entirely been placed on the 'styling' of the building envelope – a kind of branding by means of shaping, patterning and ornamentation. The resulting divorce of the logic of the building envelope from the logic of the interior is indeed celebrated by some, such as Sylvia Lavin, who writes: 'The skin is free from formal and expressive obligations to the interior … .'[2] Whatever design process these projects follow, the reality of such schemes is that architects sculpt the exterior, while the interior tends to consist of unrelated and often quite normative solutions. Thus the idiosyncratic architectural project has progressively become one of a sculptural *total exterior*. Context remains largely ignored in such works. So-called signature architectures are principally exchangeable, irrespective of differences in location, culture and climate, and it is add-on technology that typically is employed to compensate. Ironically the accelerating multiplication of the idiosyncratic converts it progressively into a *new generic*: the spectacular is absorbed back into monotonous normality by way of incessant replication. Such works bear little projective power relative to a specific situation or context precisely because of their increasing exchangeability and literal superficiality.

A more general trend also enhances discreteness in a significant way. Current approaches in sustainable design that focus predominantly on technical solutions tend to enhance the division of interior from exterior environments. Great efforts are invested in the development of more efficient building insulation and technological regulation of environmental exchange between interior and exterior. In this context it is easily overlooked that technology-dominated solutions are a rather recent phenomenon. From the 1960s onwards, mechanical-electrical interior climate modulation redefined the architectural boundary as a quasi-hermetic flattened one that has progressively abandoned intermediary spaces as architectural means of environmental provision and potential for adaptive habitation. This development prompted Kenneth Frampton to diagnose that:

> Modern building is now so universally conditioned by optimised technology
> that the possibility of creating significant urban form has become extremely
> limited … Today the practice of architecture seems so increasingly
> polarised between, on the one hand, a so-called 'high-tech' approach

predicated exclusively upon production and, on the other, the provision of a 'compensatory facade' to cover up the harsh realities of this universal system.[3]

While interesting concepts have gradually emerged that operate on notions such as free-running (non-air-conditioned) buildings and 'adaptive models of thermal comfort',[4] detailed discussions of heterogeneous and gradient conditioning of building-related microclimates are lacking. The majority of architects have at this stage not recognised the potential of such developments or incorporated them into their work. Instead the general trend is to favour pre-calculated technical solutions that secure swift planning approval and avoid the need for costly research and the associated production of reliable data. Moreover, clients today generally expect the maximum available footprint of a project to be defined as a fully climate-controlled interior, minus the necessary thickness of the climate envelope.

One of the most fundamental consequences of the dominance of objectness and discreteness in architecture is that it is thereby locked into the stringent dialectic of the natural versus the man-made. There is no real option for a more subtle and graded relation that would allow architecture extensively to participate in a wide range of interlinked environmental and ecological processes, rather than being limited to technologically facilitated exchanges. Architects are hence in need of reconsidering their preoccupation with discreteness.

Nevertheless, some works begin to point in a direction that might be considered non-discrete architecture. In reference to his own work and that of Bruno Taut, the Japanese architect Kengo Kuma demanded in his book *Anti-Object* that architects must 'shun the stability, unity and aggregation known as the object'.[5] He went on to state that 'making architecture into an object means distinguishing between its inside and outside and erecting a mass called "inside" in the midst of an "outside" (of which nature is one version)'.[6] The following four types of works present alternative strategies.

Firstly, the oeuvre of the Brazilian architect Paulo Mendes da Rocha features a series of projects that extensively engage the ground in the formation of the architecture and thereby extend the space of the project beyond its actual footprint. Examples of this design approach include the Brazilian Pavilion for the Osaka Expo 1970 and MUBE – the Brazilian Museum of Sculpture in São Paulo (1988) – both of which constitute in some way constructed landscapes and are not actually immediately recognisable as buildings with interior space. The latter is set into the constructed landscape and the

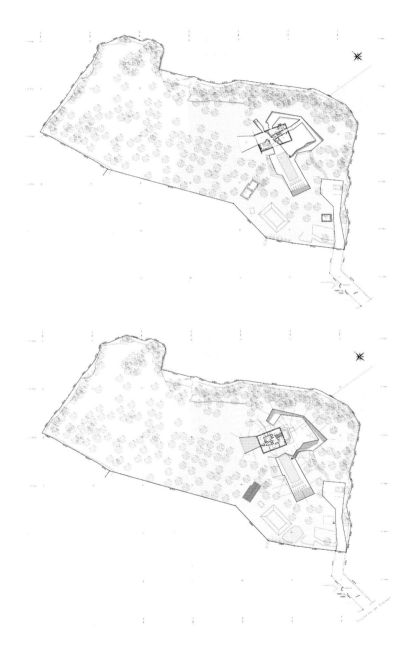

034

landscaped surface continues in an articulated manner over the 'burrowed' interior. In both cases a visible structure frames the site to a greater or lesser extent. In the case of the Brazilian Pavilion this is a concrete slab forming a canopy, while in the case of MUBE it is a very large beam. These light shelters captivatingly enhance the notion of the constructed landscape and emphasise by virtue of a 'compressed' space the horizontal extent of space the project engages. Interestingly, MUBE was initially thought to combine a sculpture and ecology museum, and was thus planned from the onset as a landscape with integrated gardens, water-pools, etc, designed by the Brazilian landscape designer Roberto Burle Marx. This kind of architecture can no longer be described as a figure-ground relation. It renders space as particularised yet continuous, and architecture as non-discrete.

As a second example, Elizabeth Diller and Ricardo Scofidio's Blur building for the Swiss Expo 2002 located in Yverdon-les-Bains on Lake Neuchâtel was, according to the architects, conceived as an 'anti-spectacle' characterised by a building envelope that is entirely dissolved into a technology-generated cloud-shaped mist of water. The project constitutes a dynamic climatic event that is affected by the climate around it rather than a rigid material construct. The physicality of the building consists of the microclimate it creates and in this way engages an extreme version of non-discreteness. In so doing it resonates with Reyner Banham's notion of the campfire as a nomadic paradigm of spatial organisation:

> Societies who do not build substantial structures tend to group their activities around some central focus – a water hole, a shade tree, a fire, a great teacher – and inhabit a space whose external boundaries are vague, adjustable according to functional need, and rarely regular. The output of heat and light from a campfire is effectively zoned in concentric rings, brightest and hottest close to the fire, coolest and darkest away from it … but at the same time, the distribution of heat is biased by the wind … so that the concentric zoning is interrupted by other considerations of comfort or need.[7]

A third strategy is presented by François Roche and Stéphanie Lavaux's Spidernethewood project in Nîmes, France (2007), which utilises dense greenery to mask the massing of the building together with its elevations, but maintains a spatial labyrinth by employing nets to limit the growth of the natural vegetation. The spatial labyrinth is designed as a continuum across the interior–exterior threshold. It would seem that François Roche and Stéphanie Lavaux responded to Kengo Kuma's assertion that 'if we are to achieve more open spaces, we must aim for a wilderness rather than a garden'.[8] Yet, although Kuma advocated giving up 'paths that are determined by their designers',[9] the Spidernethewood project clearly features determined paths, thresholds and spatial continuities. It does so, however, in a convoluted labyrinthine manner that erases any perception of determined sequence and suggests instead a maze carved within barely restrained vegetation. And although the scheme does have clear separations between an inside and an outside, it doubles it up into the net-restrained interior carved out of the vegetation (which is at the same time its exterior), its continuation in the carved interior of the barely perceivable actual building mass.

The fourth type of project spreads the boundaries and thresholds that would define the discrete object into a series of layers. This approach coincides with what Jeffrey Kipnis referred to as a *box-in-box section*

Opposite: R&Sie(n), Spidernethewood, Nîmes, France, 2007
Top: The dense vegetation of the site masks the Spidernethewood project. Centre: Nets and vegetation combine to form an exterior space with a porous border. The transition from exterior to interior is clearly defined, while the space articulated by the net on the exterior and the textile surfaces of the interior is continuous and geometrically congruent. Bottom: Various views of the 'carved' and continuous interior space.

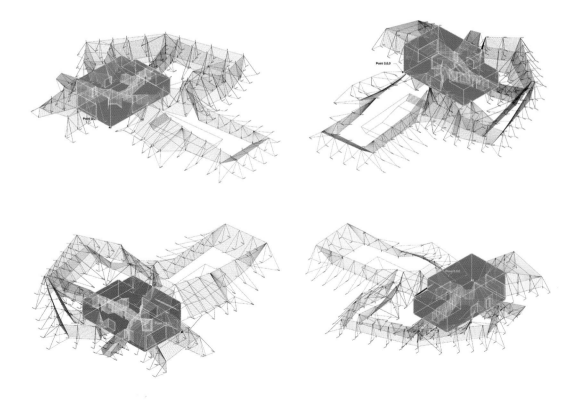

that constitutes degrees of interiority.[10] However, here it is important to distinguish between two different types of projects: one that features a continuous outer envelope and one that does not. Examples of the former include Jean Nouvel's unbuilt scheme for the New National Theatre in Tokyo (1986) and Bahram Shirdel's unbuilt entry for the Nara Convention Centre competition (1993). The latter include, for instance, Bernard Tschumi's Le Fresnoy Art Centre in Tourcoing, France (1991–7) and Steven Holl's unbuilt entry to the Palazzo del Cinema Venice competition (1990). The first type of project maintains a strong emphasis on the objectness

Opposite: R&Sie(n), Spidernethewood, Nîmes, France, 2007
The axonometrics of the Spidernethewood project show the 'carved' building volume and its continuation in the exterior space defined by nets.

of the scheme: it is the outer envelope, perceived from the exterior, that also clearly divides interior from exterior, in spite of the degrees of interiority experienced in the interior. The second type of project distributes the threshold by not pursuing a full enclosure with the outer layer: the exterior extends beyond the first layer of the multiplied envelope. The cited projects nevertheless end up emphasising the objectness of the scheme as recognisable signature buildings of the architect. They point, however, in an interesting direction that implies a further distribution of the exterior-to-interior transition by increasing the number of layers that are partially or fully open with interstitial modulated microclimates that can constitute a varied or gradient environment.

From these examples it is possible to extract a first set of principles towards an intensively embedded non-discrete architecture:

1 Architectures can be embedded in a continuous landscape with gradual transitions from exterior to interior. Through a committed engagement with landscape, architectures can be embedded in pedospheric (soil regime), hydrospheric (water regime) and biotic (organism regime) processes.

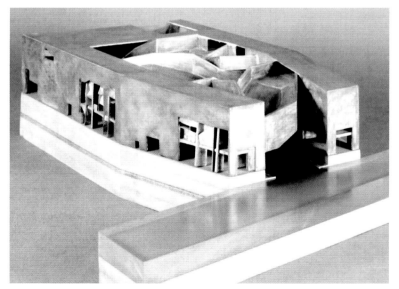

Steven Holl, Palazzo del Cinema, Venice, Italy, 1990
The model of Steven Holl's unbuilt entry to the Palazzo del Cinema Venice competition shows the partially open perimeter of the building volume that supports the three suspended theatres. This scheme offers an extended transition from exterior to interior.

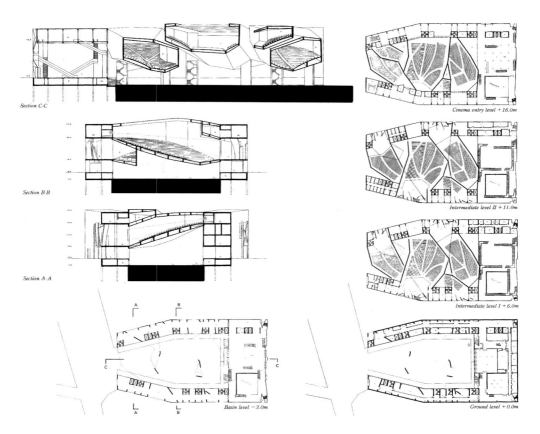

Section C-C

Cinema entry level +16.0m

Section B-B

Intermediate level II +11.0m

Section A-A

Intermediate level I +6.0m

Basin level −3.0m

Ground level +0.0m

Steven Holl, Palazzo del Cinema, Venice, Italy, 1990
The sections and plans of the Palazzo del Cinema Venice scheme show the varying relations and transitions between exterior and interior space of this version of a box-in-box section.

2 Architectures are always already participating in atmospheric processes and the production of heterogeneous microclimate. However, the interaction between architectures and (local) climate can be strategised in a much more complex and nuanced manner.

3 Expanding upon points 1 and 2, architectures can participate in the production of a dynamic continuous space and environment that consists of and/or provides for local ecosystems.

4 Architectures can provide distributed thresholds that articulate heterogeneous spatial and environmental conditions to make versatile provisions for habitation and ecological processes.

As these examples show, the pursuit of non-discrete architectures requires no denial of formal concerns. However, it is of critical importance to relate such concerns to the way in which architectures participate in numerous 'authored and un-authored conditions'.[11]

Moreover, it is interesting to examine the notion of non-discrete architectures relative to the object–subject relation. Architectures can engage the subject above and beyond practical purposes and can accomplish this by emphasis on being outstanding (spectacular) and/or on unfamiliarity. In this context Umberto Eco's seminal *The Open Work* is of interest, in which he described a kind of work of art that invests part of the action in the spectator.[12] Such 'open work' or 'work in movement', as Eco called it, is characterised by a deliberate ambiguity of meaning and seeks to avoid conventional forms of expression and prescribed interpretation. According to Eco, 'open works' must leave the arrangement of some of their constituents to the public or to chance, hence giving these works a 'field of possible orders' rather than a single fixed one. The subject can move freely within this field of possibilities. At the same time, Eco pointed out that this does not imply a comprehensive laissez-faire and amorphousness. Instead, the designer needs to provide a guiding directive that structures the field of possibilities in some way for the subject. Eco explained that:

> (1) 'open' works … are characterised by the invitation to *make the work* together with the author … (2) … there exist works which, though organically completed, are 'open' to a continuous generation of internal relations which the addressee must uncover and select in his act of perceiving the totality of incoming stimuli. (3) *Every* work of art … is effectively open to a virtually unlimited range of possible readings, each of which causes the work to acquire new vitality in terms of particular taste, or perspective, or personal *performance*.[13]

'Open works' are therefore based on the active agency of the subject. The question is how such 'openness' can be devised? The author of a work could, for instance, accomplish this by saturating it with meaning or operate on displacements of meaning. This approach is problematic for two reasons: firstly, the cultural specificity of meaning limits experiences of such a kind to preferred subjects; and secondly, if Kipnis's aforementioned critique of Post-Modern collage stands (see chapter 2), the approach becomes empty through repetition and the increasing replacement of a dominant frame upon which such collages rely. A second option is the reduction of meaning through forms of abstraction. This might also be culturally specific; but, if it inspires curiosity and causes the subject to actively engage and participate in the built environment in order to discover actual and latent provisions or new potentials, an interesting situation arises.[14]

Kipnis's notions of 'blankness' and 'pointing' in architecture are of interest in relation to the concept of open works. According to Kipnis, blankness implies 'the suppression of quotation or reference through the erasure of decoration and ornament to include canonic form and type. By avoiding formal or figurative reference, architecture can engage in unexpected formal and semiotic affiliations without entering into fixed alignments.'[15] Pointing implies that 'architecture must be projective, i.e., it must point to the emergence of new social arrangements and to the construction of new institutional forms. In order to accomplish this, the building must have a point, i.e., project a transformation of a prevailing political context.'[16] Blankness and pointing extends Eco's notion of open works in an interesting way by suggesting that architecture can structure a field of possibility and, in so doing, can point towards 'new social arrangements' and 'institutional form'. However, through repetition, blankness too becomes canonical form. Thus the problem may be restated not as one of blankness versus meaning, but instead as one of the articulation of division, or more specifically the seams between elements and thresholds between spaces.

The aforementioned Brazilian Pavilion designed by Paulo Mendes da Rocha for the Osaka World Expo in 1970 is worth re-examining in this context. The project constituted a constructed undulating landscape roofed over by a canopy that mirrored the undulation of the ground. Typical for da Rocha is the construction of abstract landform architecture that frames and condenses the expanse of exterior space, and particularises space locally. A small ramp led to the required utilities below ground, the only actual interior space of the project. Openings in the canopy enabled shifting bands of sunlight to animate the constructed landscape surface. The local particularisation of an otherwise continuous space by way of engaging the spatial and material articulation of the project and its interaction with the environment can thus render a project non-discrete. However, attention must also be paid to the way in which the project meets its context. In the case of the Brazilian Pavilion, this entailed the articulation of the surface of the constructed landscape to that beyond it.

For the sake of argument, we may consider three different versions of Paulo Mendes da Rocha's Brazilian Pavilion: the first version clearly demarcates the extent of the constructed landscape by changing materiality and coloration of the ground surface at the border of the plot; the second version continues the surface material and coloration of the context throughout the project; and the third version features a gradual change in the materiality and coloration of the ground surface from the plot border towards the particularised space. These three versions would be perceived in quite different ways. The first version emphasises the discreteness and objectness of the scheme in spite of the existence of a continuous space, based on the perception of a hard edge of the unfamiliar object placed against a familiar context in a typical collage manner. The second version operates on the perception of some kind of unfamiliar contraction of the familiar context. The third version operates on the perception of a gradual movement from the familiar to the unfamiliar. Each of these perceptions would be fundamentally different. The first adheres to the logic of discreteness, while the second and the third erode this perception and offer two distinct versions of non-discrete architecture, at the same time maintaining the key element of the unfamiliar.

However, this does not imply that architects should no longer design discrete spaces of any description. Architectures may feature box-in-box sections in which discrete pockets of space can be embedded within more continuous space, such as in Steven Holl's Palazzo del Cinema or R&Sie(n)'s Spidernethewood project. This indicates that hard thresholds and spatial partitioning can exist in schemes that are at the same time seamlessly embedded within their context and that feature different kinds and degrees of gradients or extended threshold conditions.

References

1 C Alexander, *Notes on the Synthesis of Form*, Harvard University Press (Cambridge, MA), 1964, p 18.

2 S Lavin, 'Performing the Contemporary, or: Towards an Even Newer Architecture', in Y Grobman and E Neuman (eds), *Performalism: Form and Performance in Digital Architecture*, Routledge (London), 2012, pp 21–6 (p 25).

3 K Frampton, 'Towards a Critical Regionalism: Six Points for an Architecture of Resistance', in H Foster (ed), *The Anti-Aesthetic: Essays on Postmodern Culture*, Bay Press (Port Townsend, WA), 1983, pp 16–30 (p 17).

4 See: RJ de Dear and GS Brager, 'Towards an Adaptive Model of Thermal Comfort and Preference', *ASHRAE Transactions*, Vol 104, No 1, 1998, pp 145–67.

5 K Kuma, *Anti-Object: The Dissolution and Disintegration of Architecture*, AA Publications (London), 2008, p 120.

6 Ibid, p 77.

7 R Banham, *The Architecture of the Well-Tempered Environment*, University of Chicago Press (Chicago, IL) / The Architectural Press (London), 1969, pp 19–20.

8 Kuma, *Anti-Object*, op cit, p 112.

9 Ibid.

10 J Kipnis, 'Towards a New Architecture', in G Lynn (ed), *Folding in Architecture – AD*, Vol 63, No 3–4, 1993, pp 40–9 (p 44).

11 D Leatherbarrow, *Architecture Oriented Otherwise* – lecture at the Oslo School of Architecture and Design, 28 April 2011.

12 U Eco, *The Open Work*, Harvard University Press (Cambridge, MA), 1989; originally published as U Eco, *Opera Aperta*, Gruppo Editoriale Fabbri, Bompiani, Sonzogno, Etas (Milan), 1962.

13 Ibid, p 21.

14 See: M Hensel, 'Re: Cognition – Approaching the Generative Function of the Unfamiliar', in P Van Loocke and Y Joye (eds), *Organic Aesthetics and Generative Methods in Architectural Design – Communication & Cognition*, Vol 36, No 3–4, 2003, pp 243–61.

15 J Kipnis, 'Towards a New Architecture', op cit, p 43.

16 Ibid.

4

Non-Anthropocentric Architectures

'The altered environmental conditions of today can no longer be mastered with the architectural resources of the past … The relationship between biology and building is now in need of clarification due to real and practical exigencies. The problem of environment has never before been such a threat to existence. In effect, it is a biological problem.'[1]

Frei Otto, 1971

'Overpopulation, the destruction of the environment, and the malaise of the inner cities cannot be solved by technological advances, nor by literature or history, but ultimately only by measures that are based on an understanding of the biological roots of these problems.'[2]

Ernst Mayr, 1997

For several decades numerous politicians, biologists and architects have stated the need for a biological approach to some of the most pressing problems arising from the extensive impact of humankind on the natural environment. The 1987 report of the World Commission on Environment and Development, entitled *Our Common Future* and commonly known as the Brundtland Report, explored a broad range of sustainability concerns, including the fundamental necessity of preserving the abiotic (non-living) and biotic (living) environment and its associated processes:

> important are the vital life processes carried out by nature, including stabilization of climate, protection of watersheds and soil, preservation of nurseries and breeding grounds, and so on. Conserving these processes cannot be divorced from conserving the individual species within natural ecosystems. Managing species and ecosystems together is clearly the most rational way to approach the problem.[3]

But how are natural processes and ecosystems to be maintained? And what kind of disciplinary affiliation between architecture and biology is needed in order to tackle the complexity of the problems arising from the interaction between the human-made and the natural environment? To confront these issues, it is necessary to focus all efforts on the question as to how the built environment can be *in the service of* the natural environment. For this a much more direct approach is needed that focuses on how architectures can progressively be thought of as being embedded in natural processes, and on how ecosystems may be protected by way of mediating the interaction between the abiotic and biotic environment. This requires clarification and integration of core concepts in architecture and biology so as to inform the integrated spatial and material organisation of architecture and its interaction with the physical environments, in order to provide the specific conditions that are needed to sustain local ecosystems and biodiversity.

Engaging architecture in the service of the natural environment concerns questions of *ecology* – a sub-discipline of biology set forth in the mid-19th century by the German biologist Ernst Haeckel that concerns the relationship between living organisms and their environment.[4] Today ecology comprises studies across a wide range of spatial and temporal scales concerning life processes and adaptation, distribution and abundance of organisms, the relation of material and energetic processes to living communities, function and development of ecosystems, and the role of biodiversity in ecosystem functioning.

The sum of all ecosystems constitutes the *biosphere*, a concept devised in the later 19th century by the geologist Eduard Suess who also coined the notions of *hydrosphere* and *lithosphere*.[5] Gordon Dickinson and Kevin Murphy have argued that the biosphere 'is located at the junction of the three terrestrial "spheres" or shells around the planet: the atmosphere, hydrosphere and lithosphere', yet 'the dynamic nature of the physical environment is not the only reason why ecosystems are dynamic. Organisms must react to the challenges and opportunities of the physical environment as well as interact with other organisms.'[6] Generally ecosystems are defined as communities of organisms and related physical conditions and processes within a specific environment. They constitute hierarchical systems of perpetually interacting agents that accumulate into a complex integrated whole, which is characterised by emergent non-reducible properties. Ecosystems generate *biophysical feedback* between living and non-living domains and are sustained by *biodiversity*. The latter indicates the extent of genetic, taxonomic and ecological diversity over all spatial and temporal scales.[7] Shahid Naeem, Michel Loreau and Pablo Inchausti have pointed out that:

> Through the collective metabolic and growth activities of its trillions of organisms, Earth's biota moves hundreds of thousands of tons of elements and compounds between the hydrosphere, atmosphere, and lithosphere every year. It is this biogeochemical activity that determines soil fertility, air and water quality, and the habitability of ecosystems, biomes and Earth itself … While the functional significance of Earth's biota to ecosystem or Earth-system functioning is well established, the significance of Earth's biodiversity has remained unknown until today.[8]

While research into the significance of biodiversity in ecosystem functioning continues, numerous industries – including pharmaceutical and agrochemical industries, agriculture, forestry and so on – have begun to incorporate biodiversity considerations into their operations.[9]

Interlinked with the notion of *biodiversity* is *geodiversity*, which concerns the diversity of earth materials, forms and processes that constitute and shape the abiotic environment. This involves water, soil, sediments and minerals, geomorphology and geological processes. It is generally thought that geology asserts a strong influence on biodiversity.[10] This comprises also the *pedospheric* regime, which concerns soil and soil formation. The latter is of particular importance for the biotic linkages and interactions between above-ground and below-ground communities.[11] Moreover, the interaction between the biotic and abiotic environment entails biogeochemical cycles (carbon, nitrogen, oxygen, phosphorus, sulphur and water cycles) that need to be considered.

Today ecologists and experts in environmental studies work with different kinds of models to simulate different aspects of ecosystems, abiotic processes or linkages between the two respectively. Often, however, key terminology is used in an ambiguous manner and requires clarification. Zoologist Michael Kearney pointed out that 'fundamental ecological concepts including "habitat", "environment" and "niche" lack rigorous and consistent definitions'.[12] For the purposes of this book, we will rely on Roger Lincoln, Geoff Boxshall and Paul Clark's *A Dictionary of Ecology, Evolution and Systematics*.[13] Here, *habitat* is defined as 'the locality, site and particular type of local environment occupied by an organism'.[14] *Environment* is defined as 'the complex of biotic, climatic, edaphic (pertaining to, or influenced by, the nature of the soil) and other conditions, which comprise the immediate habitat of an organism; the physical, chemical and biological surroundings of an organism at any given time'.[15] The concept of the *niche* is defined as '[t]he ecological role of a species in a community; conceptualised as the multidimensional space, of which the coordinates are the various parameters representing the condition of existence of the species; sometimes used loosely as an equivalent of microhabitat in the sense of the physical space occupied by a species'.[16] Moreover, it is necessary to distinguish between the notions of fundamental niche and realised niche. A *fundamental niche* is defined as '[t]he entire multidimensional space that represents the total range of conditions within which an organism can function and which it could occupy in the absence of competitors or other interacting species'.[17] A *realised niche* is defined as 'that part of the fundamental niche actually occupied by a species in the presence of competitive or interactive species'.[18] These definitions describe a successively more tightly defined space of interaction and can be useful in communication between biologists and architects when setting out what kinds of parameters are concerned at various levels of specificity, as well as developing integrated modelling towards a built environment in the service of the natural environment.

In order to gain an understanding as to how the built environment might interact with the natural environment, it is useful to consider current approaches that are specific to other types of human-dominated environments and their relation to the natural environment. One interesting field in this context is contemporary agroecosystems management, a field in which experts have begun to hypothesise 'that under conditions of global change, complex agricultural systems are more dependable in production and more sustainable in terms of resource conservation than simple ones'.[19] In this context, 'complex systems' refers to multi-species agroecosystems, while 'simple systems' refers to those tending towards monoculture. In relation to complex systems, biologist and ecologist John Vandermeer and his co-researchers differentiate between planned biodiversity, associated biodiversity and associated component, and go on to explain:

> The planned biodiversity will give rise to an associated biodiversity, the host of weeds and beneficial plants that arrive independently of the farmer's plans, the soil flora and fauna that may respond to particular crops planted, the myriad arthropods that arrive on the farm, etc. Finally, the extra-planned organic resources, plus the planned biodiversity plus the associated biodiversity combine in a complicated fashion to produce the ultimate agroecosystem function, its productivity and sustainability.[20]

What is of interest for architecture is the immediacy of planned and associated biodiversity in agroecological contexts where 'multi-species cultivation clearly necessitates biodiversity management on the plot-scale. It also, however, requires consideration of its biogeographical context within the surrounding area, requiring recognition of processes operating on various scales.'[21]

Developments in this field can therefore deliver ways of managing the correlation between planned and evolving aspects in ecosystems and their associated biodiversity, and can also deliver general models for integrating the various scales involved in human influence and natural processes interactions. Consequently, a useful inroad to the formulation of a non-anthropocentric architecture does not necessarily involve highly detailed provisions for the entire scope of biodiversity of a given ecosystem, but, instead, the integration of provisions for planned biodiversity that can help sustain an associated biodiversity and, in turn, sustain the freely evolving one.

This approach may be useful in dealing with another complex problem. Commonly ecosystem conservationists consider ecosystems to be in a state of *dynamic equilibrium*, which tends to lead to the protection of species and ecosystems in the condition in which they were found and described. The German zoologist, ecologist and evolutionary scientist Josef Helmut Reichholf criticises this approach for its failure to sufficiently incorporate evolutionary processes or the possibility of natural extinction, as maintained equilibrium entails rigid maintenance of the found condition; he proposes instead the notion of *stabile disequilibria*.[22]

Another considerable interdisciplinary effort that is of interest is the field of *urban ecology*, which involves:

> the study of ecosystems that include humans living in cities and urbanising landscapes. It is an emerging, interdisciplinary field that aims to understand how human and ecological processes can co-exist in human-dominated systems and help societies with their efforts to become more sustainable … Because of its interdisciplinary nature and unique focus on humans and natural systems, the term 'urban ecology' has been used variously to describe the study of humans in cities, of nature in cities, and the coupled relationship between humans and nature. Each of these areas is contributing to our understanding of urban ecosystems and must be understood to fully grasp the science of Urban Ecology.[23]

For the field of urban ecology, the steep task is to come to an understanding of the complexities involved at larger scales and to study the impact of mosaics of heterogeneous and discontinuous spaces from the periphery to the centre of cities. The involved conceptualisation, analysis, evaluation and incorporation of the understandings that arise from urban ecology research into urban design can either develop along an anthropocentric trajectory or along a non-anthropocentric one. While the former seems more likely, the latter might constitute a powerful alternative.

Experiments on an urban and regional scale are risky in that the result can be disastrous on a large scale, while experimentation towards multi-species environments on the scale of one or a few buildings may equally go wrong but might contain the consequences of potentially negative outcomes. Experiments geared towards non-anthropocentric architectures could therefore be locally conducted on a building scale and carefully increased in size for as long as the observed results are deemed positive. Evidently, such experiments would entail an intensely interdisciplinary approach that necessitates the involvement of architects, climatologists and microclimatologists, geologists, botanists, zoologists, ecologists, and also urban ecologists and agroecosystems experts. The concept of non-discrete architectures might provide the extended threshold or interface that is required to negotiate multi-species provisions, including of course those for human inhabitants.

References

1 F Otto, *Biology and Building, Part 1* (IL series, Vol 3), University of Stuttgart (Stuttgart), 1971, p 7.
2 E Mayr, *This is Biology: The Science of the Living World*, Belknap / Harvard University Press (Cambridge, MA), 1997, p xix.
3 *Report of the World Commission on Environment and Development: Our Common Future*, 1987, transmitted to the General Assembly as an Annex to *Document A/42/427 – Development and International Co-operation: Environment*, Chapter 6: 'Species and Ecosystems: Resources for Development' (online: http://www.un-documents.net/ocf-06.htm#I [accessed 3 December 2011]).
4 E Haeckel, *Generelle Morphologie der Organismen*, Georg Reimer (Berlin), 1866.
5 E Suess, *Das Antlitz der Erde* (*The Face of the Earth*) [1883–1909], Vol 3, Nabu Press (Charleston, SC), 2010.
6 G Dickinson and K Murphy, *Ecosystems*, second edition, Routledge (London), 2007, pp 6–7.
7 JL Harper and DL Hawksworth, *Biodiversity: Measurement and Estimation*, Chapman & Hall (Oxford), 1995.

8 S Naeem, M Loreau and P Inchausti, 'Biodiversity and Ecosystem Functioning: The Emergence of a Synthetic Ecological Framework', in M Loreau, S Naeem and P Inchausti (eds), *Biodiversity and Ecosystem Functioning: Synthesis and Perspectives*, Oxford University Press (Oxford), 2002, p 3.
9 See, for example: S Wrigley, M Hayes, R Thomas, EJT Chrystal and N Nicholson (eds), *Biodiversity: New Leads for the Pharmaceutical and Agrochemical Industries*, Royal Society of Chemistry (Cambridge), 2000; JA McNeely and SJ Scherr, *Ecoagriculture: Strategies to Feed the World and Save Wild Biodiversity*, Island Press (Washington DC), 2002; FL Bunnell and GB Dunsworth, *Forestry and Biodiversity: Learning How To Sustain Biodiversity In Managed Forests*, UBC Press (Vancouver; Toronto), 2009.
10 See: M Gray, *Geodiversity: Valuing and Conserving Abiotic Nature*, John Wiley & Sons (Chichester), 2004.
11 See: RD Bardgett and DA Wardle, *Aboveground–Belowground Linkages: Biotic Interactions, Ecosystem Processes, and Global Change*, Oxford University Press

(Oxford), 2010.
12 M Kearney, 'Habitat, Environment and Niche: What Are We Modelling?', *Oikos*, Vol 115, No 1, 2006, pp 186–91 (p 186).
13 R Lincoln, G Boxshall and P Clark, *A Dictionary of Ecology, Evolution and Systematics*, second edition, Cambridge University Press (Cambridge), 1998.
14 Ibid, p 132.
15 Ibid, p 101.
16 Ibid, p 201.
17 Ibid, p 121.
18 Ibid, p 256.
19 J Vandermeer, M van Noordwijk, J Anderson, C Ong and I Perfecto, 'Global Change and Multi-Species Agroecosystems: Concepts and Issues', *Agricultures, Ecosystems and Environment*, Vol 67, 1998, pp 1–22 (p 4).
20 Ibid, p 6.
21 Ibid.
22 JH Reichholf, *Stabile Ungleichgewichte – Die Ökologie der Zukunft*, Suhrkamp (Frankfurt), 2008.
23 JM Marzluff, E Shulenberger, W Endlicher, M Alberti, G Bradley, C Ryan, U Simon and C ZumBrunnen (eds), *Urban Ecology: An International Perspective on the Interaction between Humans and Nature*, Springer (New York), 2008.

5

Traits of Performance-Oriented Architecture

The concept of non-discrete embedded architectures yields questions as to what the conditions are that architectures are to engage in, how architectures should partake in specific settings, and how to devise appropriate design approaches and methods. These questions are profoundly linked to the issue of sustainability. Paul Reitan, Professor Emeritus of Geological Sciences at the University of Buffalo, called for sustainable human societies that need to be:

> as attuned as possible to their local and regional environments, their geo-ecological support systems; lifestyles must be adapted to the ecosystems in which societies live and which support them with cultures, practices, economic systems, and governing policies each adjusted to fit their area … This would be a world of multiple, diverse societies with their numbers also adjusted to what regional geo-ecological support systems can sustain.[1]

For architecture, this implies the significance of complex context-specific relations across a range of scales and in particular according to geo-ecological conditions. Local factors should generate different architectural responses. The emphasis on context-specificity does not, however, simply imply a return to Kenneth Frampton's 'Critical Regionalism', as Frampton's approach does not necessarily require non-discrete or non-anthropocentric architectures.[2] Sanford Kwinter, Professor of Architectural Theory and Criticism at the Harvard University Graduate School of Design, offered a useful conceptual repositioning regarding what architectures *are* and what they *do*:

Thus the object – be it a building, a compound site, or an entire urban matrix
… – would be defined now *not by how it appears, but rather by practices*:
those it partakes of and those that take place within it … those relations
that are smaller than the object, that saturate it and compose it, the 'micro-
architectures' … and … those relations or systems that are greater or more
extensive than the object, that comprehend or envelope it, those 'macro-
architectures' of which the 'object' … is but a relay member or part.[3]

What kinds of relations and 'practices' might be involved in each case and
to what extent requires careful attention. In approaching this question, a
systems approach can help to define the extent of relevant interactions
to be included in architectural design considerations and processes. This
becomes even more important when considering the impact of humans
on the transformation of Earth's biosphere: experts now posit that we
have entered a new geological age dominated by human intervention.
Nobel-prize laureate and chemist Paul Crutzen argued that our geological
time period should be termed 'Anthropocene', as 'human activity is now
affecting the Earth so profoundly that we are entering into a new epoch'.[4]
This view alerts us to the fact that human actions are not only adding up,
but might have passed a critical threshold.

When consequences are so far reaching, it is far from straightforward to
identify which considerations should inform an appropriate architectural
response. This classical challenge is known to systems-thinkers as the 'boundary
problem'. It involves what is included in or excluded from architectural design
considerations, and requires knowledge also of those aspects that are to be
excluded. Where the boundary is drawn is of key significance, as this will
influence how a given problem is understood and dealt with.[5] As Werner Ulrich
pointed out, 'the meaning and the validity of professional propositions always
depend on *boundary* judgments as to what "facts" (observations) and "norms"
(valuation standards) are to be considered relevant and what others are to
be left out or considered less important'.[6] For the task at hand this implies
the involvement of an interdisciplinary range of experts who define borders
perpetually according to circumstances. A valuable clue as to how to address
the problem of complex relation vis-à-vis questions of sustainability was offered
by Pim Martens, professor and chair of Global Dynamics and Sustainable
Development at Maastricht University, who suggested that:

A new research paradigm is needed that is better able to reflect the complexity
and the multidimensional character of sustainable development. The new

paradigm, referred to as sustainability science, must be able to encompass different magnitudes of scales (of time, space, and function), multiple balances (dynamics), multiple actors (interests) and multiple failures (systemic faults).[7]

In so doing he calls for a new research paradigm for 'Sustainability Science'. William C Clark, co-director of the Sustainability Science Program at Harvard University, explained that 'fundamental properties of the complex, adaptive human–environment systems … are the heart of sustainability science'.[8] Performance-oriented architecture can benefit from a disciplinary affiliation with sustainability science in that human–environment systems are shared core interests.

One of the core areas of architectural production is the combined spatial and material organisation of a project by which architecture makes provisions. Capacity for *active agency* on a range of scales is inherent to the domains of spatial and material organisation. As these two domains are interdependent it is of use to view them as a combined *spatial and material organisation complex*. This complex interacts with the local environment: it receives stimuli from the environment and modulates it in turn. The locally modulated environment is an integral part of the spatial organisation of architectures and can have a supporting or diminishing effect on local ecosystems and cultural patterns. Therefore it seems useful to state the four domains of agency as: (i) local communities – biotic factors and interactions; (ii) the local physical environment – abiotic processes and interactions; and the (iii) spatial and (iv) material organisation complex. It is then necessary to define the different traits and scale-ranges in which the spatial and material organisation complex can be thought of and instrumentalised.

Moreover, the notion of performance-oriented architecture raises the question of causality and control. Embedded architectures will be entangled in complex multi-level interactions that make it difficult to decide what kind of multiple-ways cause-and-effect relations are to be taken into consideration, while at the same time allowing for contingent influences. Typically the complexity of a given problem is 'reduced' for the sake of intelligibility and to establish convention and ease of use. Architecture too employs reductionism for such purposes. However, the often-resulting artificial dichotomies tend stubbornly to persist in separating architectural discourses into oppositional entrenchment.

Biophysical Environment

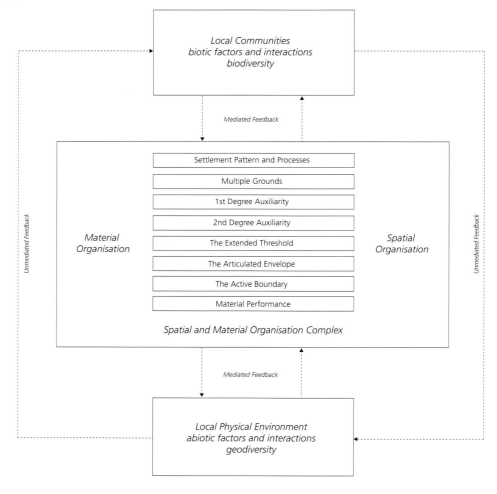

One unquestionably iconic artificial dichotomy in architecture divides *form* from *function*. The debate and disagreement on their relation has divided architects since the 1930s[9] and in some ways even before, as can be gleaned from the different positions that were informed by different takes on comparative anatomy and morphology in biology. The form–function dialectic constitutes a profound problem for an integrated perspective on performance-oriented architecture as it continues to divide architects into factions with either predominantly formal or functional predilections. What makes matters additionally difficult is the frequent general conflation firstly of the notions of *function*, *purpose*, *use* and *programme*, and secondly of the notions of *function* and *performance*. It is therefore necessary to reconcile the form–function dialectic and to provide an unambiguous definition of the related notions.

Regarding the latter purpose it is useful to shift the definition of *function* from the building scale to materials, material systems and building elements, so as to describe the way in which these fulfil their tasks and affect conditions. The notion of *programme* is shifted away from sets of activities assigned to spaces towards the participation of architectures in conditions and systems to which they are auxiliary. The notion of *space use* is maintained as the relation between spaces and activities, but with emphasis on the fact that architecture can only make *provisions* towards habitation and space use, rather than dictating them. In consequence the pursuit of single space use is relinquished. According to these definitions it is possible to state *function*, *programme* and *provision* for habitation, as some of the particular subsets of the notion of *performance*.

Local Climate and Microclimate

The biophysical environment encompasses the natural and the built environment. It combines both biotic and abiotic components. Ecosystems generate *biophysical feedback* between living and non-living domains. Architecture *in the service of* the natural environment and, more specifically, of local ecosystems, needs to engage the local physical environment. Before defining and examining the traits of performance-oriented architecture, an understanding of some fundamental aspects of climate and microclimate, and of their interaction with architecture, is therefore required.

Architecture interacts with and affects various spatial and temporal scales of atmospheric processes. However, of the very large range of scales of atmospheric phenomena, only a specific portion is of immediate relevance. As Tim R Oke pointed out, the influence of the surface of the Earth is limited to the *troposphere*, the lowest 10 kilometres of the atmosphere, of which the important part for architecture is the *atmospheric boundary layer*. The latter can vary in height between 100 metres and 2,000 metres depending on surface-generated mixing.[10] Oke defined the related climatic strata from the ground upwards: first, the laminar *boundary layer* 'which is in direct contact with the surface(s) … the non-turbulent layer, at most a few millimetres thick, that adheres to all surfaces and establishes a buffer between the surface and the more freely diffusive environment above'; second, the *roughness layer* that extends above the surface and objects about one to three times their height or spacing and that is 'highly irregular being strongly affected by the nature of the individual roughness features'; third, the *turbulent surface layer*, up to 50 metres high, that features 'intense small-scale turbulence generated by the surface roughness and convection'.[11] Moreover, the vertical extent of these strata is dynamically affected by the *atmospheric boundary layer* that is characterised by turbulences 'generated by frictional drag as the Atmosphere moves across the rough and rigid surface of the Earth, and the "bubbling-up" of air parcels from the heated surface'.[12]

A further useful difference concerns micro- and macroclimate. Norman J Rosenberg, Blaine L Blad and Shashi B Verma explain:

> Microclimate is the climate near the ground, that is, the climate in which plants and animals live. … it is the great range in environmental conditions near the surface and the rate of these changes with time and elevation that makes the microclimate so different from the climate just a few metres above, where atmospheric mixing processes are much more active and the climate is both more moderate and more stable.[13]

According to Rosenberg, Blad and Verma, local microclimates are characterised by significant daytime range in temperature, change in humidity, energy exchange and wind-speed decrease near the Earth's surface. Therefore, leaving very tall buildings aside, it is the laminar boundary layer, the roughness layer and the turbulent surface layer, as well as the microclimate, that are of immediate relevance for the bulk of architecture's interaction with the atmosphere.

Material Performance

Materials are defined by their specific composition and structure from which their properties arise. While some material properties are relatively constant, others vary due to their interaction with independent variables. One example of this is the dimensional variation that can be caused by changes in temperature or in ambient humidity. Fluctuating material properties are thus 'indicative of the energy stimuli that every material must respond to'.[14] In turn material behaviour can also affect its surroundings. Materials can absorb or reflect thermal energy and give stored thermal energy off to the environment. Hygroscopic materials such as wood can absorb moisture from the environment or yield it back, 'thereby attaining a moisture-content which is in equilibrium with the water vapour pressure of the surrounding atmosphere'.[15] Material behaviour can be put to task and constitute the potential of material performance.

While variable material properties and behaviour present an important opportunity for performance-oriented architecture, a profound obstruction to their exploitation exists in current practice. With the increase in standardisation, tight tolerances and stringent liability in the building industry, explicit and variable material behaviour and associated variable dimensionality is generally deemed a negative characteristic. Constrained by stringent

Harnessing material performance
The specific structure and composition of materials yields their properties, and, in interaction with a given environment, material behaviour. The latter constitutes material performance capacity that can be put to task. This constitutes the smallest but greatly effective scale of performance-oriented architecture.

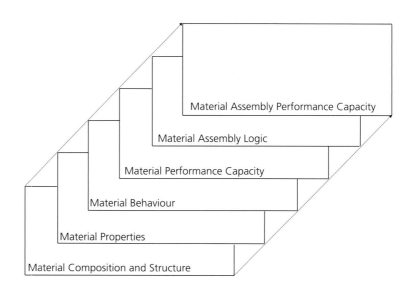

Material Assembly Performance Capacity

Material Assembly Logic

Material Performance Capacity

Material Behaviour

Material Properties

Material Composition and Structure

standards, architects principally seek to prevent or neutralise the effects of variable material behaviour on the scale of the chosen material, building component or assembly method, to avoid cumulative effects. Divergence from defined standards and pre-calculated solutions generally requires costly tests and proof for the architect and a lengthy process towards permission of use. Few practices can afford this course of action, and more often than not such efforts focus on narrowly framed applied research rather than the extensive basic research that is required for a critical repositioning of the prevailing approach to variable material behaviour and dimensionality. And so the question arises as to the context in which the necessary depth and breadth of inquiry and empirical knowledge production could take place. It would seem that such activities could currently best be undertaken in dedicated architectural research centres. However, funding and resourcing largely basic research in the current research grant environment is not an easy task. One way forward is sustained research by design that can bridge between basic research undertakings and testing by way of full-scale experiments within the target context.

To illustrate the potential of material behaviour, it is useful to discuss a specific material at some level of detail. Wood, due to its organic nature, is one of the new hallmarks and clichés of material sustainability in architecture. However, its essential characteristics – that is, its material differentiation, which results from growth-related variables, and its resultant behaviour – are often deemed undesirable. If one considers, for instance, how wood may be utilised with regards to its hygroscopic behaviour, one also needs to take into consideration all properties and characteristics that affect its response to moisture disequilibria, such as its species-specific density, anisotropy, porosity and cellular differentiation. It is, however, the material differentiation of wood that comes into conflict with the prevailing considerations concerning standardisation, tolerances and liability. This explains why the preferred mode of working with wood is moving in the direction of homogenising its behaviour by way of cutting or chipping it into smaller elements that are laminated together.

An alternative approach to the above may commence from the consideration as to how wood comes to be the way it is. The internal structure of wood depends on the circumstances under which a tree from which the wood is harvested has grown. Various recent publications give evidence of increased interest in the material differentiation of wood in relation to environment[16] and the technical innovation potentials associated with the anisotropic character of wood.[17] This implies that considerations of the environment must be twofold: first with regards to its impact on the material differentiation of wood in its growth phase, and second, the two-way exchange between the harvested wood in a designed assembly and the environment in which it is placed. The numerous variables related to the growth process can thus become a matter of design consideration, as does the resultant material behaviour based on its differentiation and heterogeneity.

If the properties of a material and its related behaviour are brought to the fore, this will have repercussions along the entire supply and demand chain. In order to develop a suitable approach, the Research Center for Architecture and Tectonics at the Oslo School of Architecture and Design pursues 'Holistic and Integrated Wood Research'. This involves the detailed mapping of related existing research and of the sustainability aspects involved across the supply and demand chain. As industrial forestry is under increasing pressure to emphasise biodiversity instead of monoculture[18] and architects seek a much broader range of available wood species and products, a promising match of interests emerges. However, the question arises as to how to reposition the intermediary parts of the wood industry such as wood sorting, treatment and machining. Likewise policy makers will need to rethink the role and extent of existing and future standards and tolerances in material behaviour. This can only be accomplished in a concerted effort that involves all stakeholders. Moreover, such efforts need to engage knowledge and skills of traditional wood craftsmanship, scientific knowledge of wood properties and behaviour and a related detailed logic of wood sorting, storage, tooling and fabrication.

Any change in the way wood properties and behaviour may be used will involve the consideration of different timelines. Clearly the change of the forestry industry from an emphasis on monocultures of spruce and pine to one focused on biodiversity will require decades, even centuries. Changes in tooling and machining will take a number of years. The enhancement of awareness through research-by-design experimentation can, however, commence with immediate effect and may need to focus on two aspects: firstly, the development of reliable data; and secondly, the production of intellectual tools and sensibilities in education to provide architects and craftsmen with the required knowledge and skills.

In the context of the 'Responsive Wood Architectures' studio at the Oslo School of Architecture and Design in 2010, Industrial Design masters student

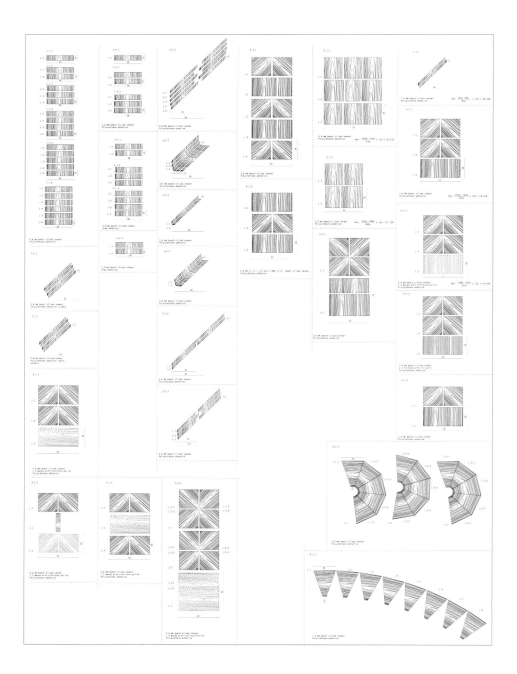

Opposite: Linn Tale Haugen, Diploma Project, Oslo School of Architecture and Design, Norway, 2010
Linn Tale Haugen's research required a series of material experiments, varying the wood type and cut, element geometry, layer number and thickness, fibre direction per layer, etc in order to use the findings in a rigorous and reliable manner and derive dependable empirical data. This chart lists the different experiments in a systematic manner.

Linn Tale Haugen examined the seed pod of a Flamboyant tree (*Delonix regia*), focusing on its material make-up and resulting self-shaping tendencies induced by hygroscopic behaviour.[19] The seed pod is characterised by a layering of material with different fibre directions. The angle of rotation of the fibres in the layers and the thickness of these layers determine the

degree of warping of the two parts of the seed pod as a result of shrinkage induced by moisture loss. The warping serves the purpose of separating the two parts of the seed pod and releasing the seeds. Based on this observation, Haugen re-examined lamination rules for form-stabile laminates. Timber laminates are generally composed of an odd number of layers since this locks the warping directions of the different layers into a form-stabile configuration. As the warping is determined by the fibre direction, the specific rotation of the layers is key to accomplishing form-stability. Likewise, however, this offers the opportunity to devise non-form-stabile laminates that exploit the hygroscopic behaviour of the material. In a laminate

Right: Linn Tale Haugen, Diploma Project, Oslo School of Architecture and Design, Norway, 2010
The diploma project of Industrial Design masters student Linn Tale Haugen focused on experimenting with non-form-stabile timber laminates. By utilising the hygroscopic behaviour of wood it is possible to employ self-shaping processes to derive double-curved panels without the use of jigs or moulds or energy- and material-consuming subtractive fabrication processes.

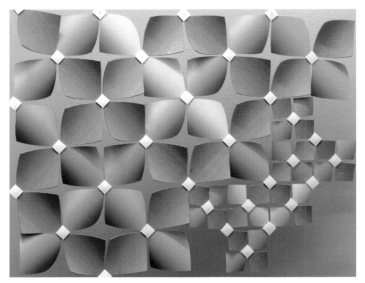

Linn Tale Haugen, Diploma Project, Oslo School of Architecture and Design, Norway, 2010
Linn Tale Haugen's research included the development of a number of design applications that utilise and benefit from the self-shaping capacity of particular wood laminates. This example shows a partial prototype for a hanging screen wall that responds to changing ambient humidity. When ambient humidity increases, the elements swell and acquire more curvature, making the screen wall more open (above left). With decreasing ambient humidity the elements shrink and straighten, resulting in a more closed screen wall (below left).

with an even number of layers, the fibre direction of the various layers can be utilised to warp the laminate in a controlled way. In addition, the degree of hygroscopic behaviour in different wood species determines their degree of warping. This then delivers control over the direction and extent of what becomes controlled warping.

Specific single or double curvature of laminates can be attained by way of fibre direction in the different layers and the related directions of swelling and shrinkage in moisturising and drying the wood. It is then no longer necessary to derive such curved elements by means of machining, such as routing, which results in a large amount of offcuts or sawdust, or, alternatively, the costly production of moulds. After numerous experiments with different types of wood, Haugen decided on using beech veneer due to its elasticity and related ability to warp without cracking. Subsequently she undertook a large number of experiments to arrive at pre-specified curvatures of the laminate. This was initially done with continuous layers, that is to say one fibre direction per layer, and subsequently with layers consisting of rotated patches to gain more surface area and more curvature variation in the laminate. The self-shaping process remains to some extent reversible when the material remains untreated. Alternatively the laminate can be fixed in the warped shape by sealing the surface. In her masters dissertation Haugen also demonstrated various applications for the process in product design, including a screen wall and a lampshade that respond to changes in the ambient humidity.

Also in the context of the 'Responsive Wood Architectures' studio, masters students Wing Yi Hui and Lap Ming Wong utilised the hygroscopic behaviour of wood too, but for a different purpose. Their goal was to work towards the structural use of 0.75-millimetre thin pine veneer in a structural web. An initial series of experiments served to establish the relationship between cut, fibre direction, moisture content and the extent to which the rectangular veneer elements could be bent and twisted without cracking. In a second series of experiments, the elements were configured into assemblies, with each element bent and twisted. A high moisture content was ensured during the assembly process. The students then examined where cracks occurred in the drying process due to the way the elements shrank in relation to one another. This eventually enabled a controlled process of assembling elements with high moisture content that, in the process of drying and shrinking, increased the tension in the assembly without cracking. The process of post-stressing due to drying increased

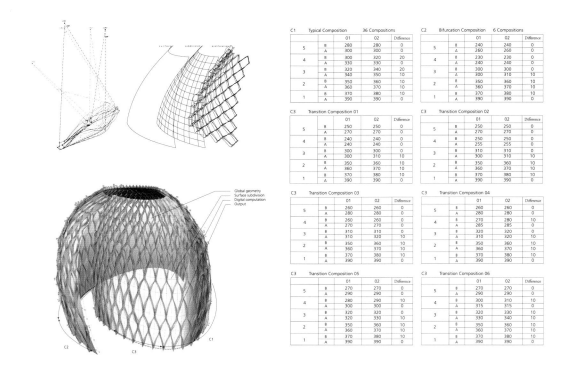

the structural capacity of the resultant structural web. This capacity was demonstrated in a full-scale construction of a small pavilion for the Oslo Architectural Triennial in 2010.

The correspondence between biological precedent and designed wood product in Linn Tale Haugen's work highlights one particular trend of learning from organic materials. The analysis of the Flamboyant tree seed pod's material composition, structure, properties and behaviour in response to extrinsic stimuli is of great use for harnessing material performance. Substantial research into organic materials has been carried out,[20] but it is not sufficiently recognised by architects as a source for innovation.

The combination of basic research and research-by-design experiments geared towards the production of reliable knowledge and re-skilling need not necessarily be confined to wood or anisotropic materials in general. Material performance and its capacity to engage and affect local microclimate are of interest for performance-oriented architecture. Considerations as to the

Wing Yi Hui and Lap Ming Wong, Responsive Wood Architectures Studio Project, Oslo School of Architecture and Design, Norway, 2010
Masters students Wing Yi Hui and Lap Ming Wong investigated the possibility of deriving structural capacity from an assembly made of 0.75-mm thin pine veneer. The associative computational modelling process is informed by an extensive series of material experiments.

microclimatic conditions of a relatively undisturbed site, or those that need to be provided for existing or desired local communities, can inform the choice of materials and their exposure and orientation in relation to thermal radiation and airflow. In the case of materials with hygroscopic behaviour, such considerations must involve the humidity regime close to the material surface. Therefore studies of different materials' capacity for microclimatic modulation in a specific context are of great interest.

The Active Architectural Boundary, the Articulated Envelope and Heterogeneous Environments

The architectural boundary is generally understood as a material partition – a floor, wall or ceiling that separates adjacent spaces or interior from exterior – while a threshold is understood as a zone between outside and inside, or one space and another, that connects and divides at the same time. Throughout architectural history and across different cultures and climate zones the articulation of the architectural boundary and threshold have varied greatly together with their symbolic connotation and functional specificity, engaging the environment and offering a broad range of degrees of connection, openness and closeness, and provisions for habitation.

Developments associated with industrialisation contributed significantly to narrowing down this spectrum, in particular articulating the building envelope as a firm division between exterior and interior together with the technical climate control, standardisation and homogenisation of interior environments. The advent of mechanical-electrical interior climate control was paralleled and enhanced by the attempt to devise closed ecological systems for space flight programmes and the design of Cold War bunkers, which reached a peak in the 1960s. Together these developments accelerated the material boundary towards a quasi-hermetic division between exterior and interior.

Reyner Banham anchored this development in architectural theory by way of his seminal book *The Architecture of the Well-Tempered Environment*.[21] In this book appeared a diagram of a tent that displayed the tent membrane as a hermetic enclosure which 'deflects' moisture, airflow or thermal radiation.[22] Thus the diagram gives no evidence of the conditions that arise out of the obvious and unavoidable degree of permeability of any tent membrane: a significant but deliberate error that idealised a desired condition. This understanding is mirrored in Banham's concept of the 'Banham bubble' which features a thin membrane that hermetically divides interior from exterior and an artificial technologically-generated interior atmosphere.

Banham showed the tent diagram together with one of a campfire to illustrate what he thought of as two historically different modes of organising space: a 'Western' one that operates through partitioning of spaces by means of physical boundaries, and a 'nomadic' one characterised by the vague boundaries of gradient conditions such as heat and light, exemplified by the campfire around which people organise themselves according to preference of exposure and social hierarchy. The stance behind these diagrams still dominates architecture today. It would seem not only that the tent diagram was inaccurate on a fundamental level, but that the dialectic of Banham's proposed division between the two modes of spatial organisation was equally so, as both together characterised architectures of many pre-industrial cultures.

Wing Yi Hui and Lap Ming Wong, Responsive Wood Architectures Studio Project, Oslo School of Architecture and Design, Norway, 2010
By increasing the contact area between the pine veneer elements, the assembly can be further post-tensioned and thereby the structural capacity can be increased.

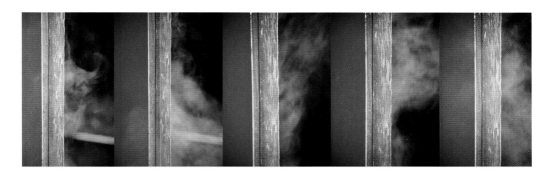

The hygroscopic behaviour of wood
This behaviour is a two-way exchange towards moisture equilibrium between the material and the environment. This sequence of photographs shows the wood releasing moisture as vapour due to the lower ambient humidity of the environment. Material behaviour such as this can modulate the microclimate.

Many other attempts to theorise the role of the envelope in orchestrating the relation between architecture and environment have been pursued since. The German philosopher Peter Sloterdijk, for instance, located the key advance in considering environment in architecture in the 19th century, when the then newly emerging hothouses or glasshouses in Great Britain aimed for the first time, in his view, at the provision of interior conditions that differed dramatically from the local environments they were placed within, so as to provide suitable conditions for alien plant species:

> Such edifices took into account that organisms and climate zones reference each other as it were a priori and that the random uprooting of organisms to plant them elsewhere could only occur if the climatic conditions were transposed along with them … It bears considering that it was the … exercise of granting plants hospitality that first created the conditions under which it became possible to formulate a concept of environment.[23]

Sloterdijk continued by pointing out the importance of Jakob von Uexküll's concept of environment:

> Not only do large stretches of modern biology depend on it but also both ecology as a whole and systems theory. If post-Uexküll the talk was of 'environment', then this meant thinking not just of the natural habitat of exotic animals and plants but also of the procedures for the technical reproduction of that habitat in alien surroundings.[24]

Sloterdijk further theorised that the invention of bent glass and prefabrication of standardised elements were key to this endeavour. Yet herein also lies the predicament: standardisation enforced its own logic onto the construction of the glasshouses, specifically repetition in structure and symmetrical volumes; and this in turn made it difficult to modulate the interior environments by architectural means in response to seasonal differences, the path and angle of the sun, prevailing wind and weather directions and so on. Instead, mechanical methods were required for these purposes. This issue also extends to the different requirements for plants that are native to very different climate zones: it was difficult to provide heterogeneous environmental conditions within one building envelope, and so separate glasshouses were built for species of more or less the same climate zone. If one compares these buildings, there is not as much difference in the architecture as one might expect. Instead, the difference lies again in the mechanical modulation of the respective interior environments. In order to control the latter it was then also necessary that the impact of all undesired exterior conditions was eliminated – instead of being put to task – thus enhancing the separation of the interior from the exterior. And, although Sloterdijk pointed out that 'we … encounter the materialisation of a new view of building by virtue of which climatic factors were taken into account in the very structure made'[25] and that this understanding continued in modern architecture, the contradictions and related shortcomings prevailed too. This is not to say that there were no interesting developments in subsequent architectures; but the contradictions were in the majority of projects reinforced instead of repositioned and solved. However, some developments of interest existed that are worth mentioning in this context.

The Open Air School Movement began to take shape in the early 1900s in Germany. Works of note emerged in the Netherlands, as well as in France. Focusing on the design of schools often for health-impaired pre-tubercular children, the movement delivered some interesting examples that foregrounded the use of exterior space and in many cases also the modulation of environment. Jan Duiker and Bernard Bijvoet's Open Air School in Amsterdam, completed in 1928, operated mainly on the principle of maximising the interface between interior and exterior. The four-storey building contained a combination of indoor and roofed-over outdoor classrooms connected by moveable parts of the building envelope and material transparency. A particularly interesting example with regards to environmental modulation is the Open Air School in Suresnes in France designed by Eugène Beaudouin and Marcel Lods and completed in 1935. This school featured south-facing freestanding classrooms aligned along a massive and opaque north wall with sufficient thermal mass, while the other three sides consisted of foldable glass elements that could be entirely retracted, thus exposing the classroom to the exterior climate. A special floor heating system made it possible to ensure a suitable temperature at seating height while at the same time providing the maximum of oxygen-rich fresh air.[26] David Leatherbarrow referred to this approach as the 'device paradigm', in which the action of the building is located in mechanically moveable parts, in the above cases as integral part of the envelope, to enable adjustment. The range of adjustability is key to 'the modification and mediation of the environment in its widest sense, from climate to human behaviour'.[27]

Generally, however, the division of homogenised interior environments from the exterior environment accelerated. A peak was reached with the development of the *Bürolandschaft* – a 1950s movement pioneered by the Quickborner Team for Planning and Organisation – which ironically intended to provide a more humane office environment. Office landscapes or *Bürolandschaften* constituted vast open-plan spaces in which clusters of workstations were arranged according to anticipated workflow. It was argued that a homogeneous interior environment minimised any visual, aural or tactile distractions, thus optimising the workflow, and a corresponding set of rules for environmental homogenisation was laid down accordingly.

These developments further intensified in the 1960s. Tight regulations for regular homogeneous interior environments were soon to follow. These were based on statistical averages and aimed at comfort and safety. The statistical averages were often based on rather predictable stereotypes and only a minimum of variations were considered in terms of degree of clothing or degree of movement relative to activity. It is hard to imagine that a specific person will have the same comfort requirements at all times and in all circumstances, and so the very basis of the preference for homogeneous interior environments seems flawed.

Interior climate control rapidly became a status symbol, and grew increasingly affordable. From the 1970s onwards, it replaced other traditional architectural means for environmental modulation throughout large parts of the world. When eventually questions of sustainability began to surface, these were invariably connected to the question of 'power-based solutions', in such a manner as to reinforce the role of technology and interior/exterior division. 'Low-' and 'zero-' energy efforts do not necessarily indicate a shift away from energy-based technology, but instead towards the least energy-consuming technologies. This constitutes today's prevailing approach in the more developed and energy-dependent countries across all climate zones, from the hot to the cold and from the humid to the dry regions of the world. In order to facilitate this approach, the architectural boundary continues to be predominantly a dividing element that is largely passively resistant, and technology constitutes the means of active exchange.

There are, however, also a number of promising approaches, among them *free-running buildings* and the *adaptive approach to thermal comfort*. Free-running buildings are not heated or cooled in general or during particular seasons. In temperate climates, for instance, a lot of buildings are not cooled or heated during the summer months. While the terminology features for the first time in regulations – such as the European Standard EN 15251: Allowing for Thermal Comfort in Free-Running Buildings – the principle itself is not new. This notion applies in general to pre-industrial buildings, and there is a fundamental difference between how climate-specific free-running buildings in the past and those of today are regarded. The adaptive approach to thermal comfort is of particular interest in this context as it begins to diverge from the strictly homogeneous interior environment regulations that have prevailed until recently. In their account of EN 15251, J Fergus Nicol and Lorenzo Pagliano explained:

> The adaptive method is a behavioural approach, and rests on the observation that people in daily life are not passive in relation to their environment, but tend to make themselves comfortable, by making adjustments (adaptations) to their clothing, activity and posture, as well as to their thermal environment. … customary temperatures (the 'comfort temperatures') are not fixed, but are subject to gradual drift in response to changes in both outdoor and indoor temperature, and are modified by climate and social custom.[28]

They continued by indicating that field research showed that daily temperature drifts of more than plus or minus 2 degrees Celsius might cause discomfort. It is interesting to note where the capacity for modifying the interior conditions is located:

> In buildings which are in free-running (FR) mode indoor conditions will follow those outdoor conditions but will be modified to a greater or lesser extent by the physical characteristics of the building and the use which building occupants make of the controls (windows, shading devices, fans etc.) which are available to them. In a successful building these actions … mean that occupants are able to remain comfortable most of the time. The function of standards is to define the indoor conditions which occupants will find agreeable for any given outdoor condition.[29]

This development is of great interest in that it informs standards by seasonal differences. The question is, however, how far local climatic conditions are considered in this set-up. Through the combination of terrain form and pronounced altitude changes, different climate zones (according to the revised Köppen–Geiger classification system), and varying wind and weather directions, local climate can vary significantly over short distances. The question therefore arises as to what extent it is feasible and useful to consider pronounced local differences.

Another aspect that is of interest is the reliance on devices to modify the interior climate. This directly relates to David Leatherbarrow's notion of a 'device paradigm', as quoted above, and raises the question whether the physical characteristics of buildings could contribute to a much larger extent and in so doing reduce the need to rely on devices. A related concern is the time-specific permissible temperature range for comfort. While this development points in an interesting direction, it prompts the question as to why a provision of concurrent heterogeneous conditions that would offer choice to the inhabitant does not feature in this approach. A great number of pre-industrial examples from different climate zones achieve this task in a resourceful manner. For the same to be possible in current architecture, the building envelope will need to be reconsidered: a single-layer, undifferentiated and flat building envelope will present severe limitations in providing a heterogeneous space and microclimate.

To start with, one may consider the architectural boundary as an active zone. The American scholars Michelle Addington and Daniel Schodek presented a useful inroad to the problem at hand by examining the notion of the boundary in other disciplines:

> For physicists … the boundary is not a thing, but an action. Environments are understood as energy fields, and the boundary operates as a transitional zone between different states of an energy field. As such it is a place of change as an environment's energy field transitions from a high-energy to low-energy state or from one form of energy to another. Boundaries are therefore, by definition, active zones of mediation rather than of delineation.[30]

Likewise Tim Oke proposed the notion of 'active' surface:

> For climatic purposes we define the 'active' surface as the principal plane of climatic activity in a system. This is the level where the majority of the radiant

energy is absorbed, reflected and emitted; where the main transformation of energy (e.g. radiant to thermal, sensible to latent) and mass (change of state of water) occur; where precipitation is intercepted; and where the major portion of drag on airflow is exerted.[31]

In the context of thermodynamics a boundary determines the relation between a thermodynamic system and its surroundings. Principally thermodynamic systems are defined by their boundary, but the exchange with their environment can vary. An open system can exchange heat, work and matter with its surroundings. A closed system can still exchange heat and work, but not matter.[32] Thus thermodynamic boundaries are not simply completely open or closed. If one considers all degrees of open and closed systems it becomes apparent that the interaction between surrounding and system will affect a spatial region to a greater or lesser degree.

The notion of the active boundary offers considerable potential for performance-oriented architecture in that it inherently involves interaction between material and environment. When an active boundary is elaborated as an architectural design it can acquire multifunctional capacities, as the following example shows.

As part of his research into the environmental modulation capacity of vernacular architecture in hot arid climates, the late Hassan Fathy analysed Islamic screen walls.[33] Known as *mashrabīyas*, these consist of wooden latticework and are characterised by a range of integrated purposes or functions: they regulate in a finely nuanced manner the passage of light, airflow, temperature and humidity of the air current, as well as visual penetration from the inside and the outside. This is accomplished by the careful calibration of the sizes of the balusters that make up the latticework and the interstices between them. Different parts of these screen walls cater for different hierarchies of the integrated functions. If, for instance, interstices need to be smaller at seating or standing height to reduce glare, the resultant reduction in airflow would be compensated for by larger interstices higher up in the latticework. From a material performance perspective, it is interesting to note the utilisation of the hygroscopic behaviour of wood towards the modulation of the humidity of the air current for the purpose of cooling:

> Wind passing through the interstices of the porous-wooden *mashrabīya* will give up some of its humidity to the wooden balusters if they are cool at night. When the *mashrabīya* is directly heated by sunlight, this humidity is released

into any air that may be flowing through the interstices … The balusters and interstices of the *mashrabīya* have optimal absolute and relative sizes that are based on the area of the surfaces exposed to the air and the rate at which the air passes through. Thus if the surface area is increased by increasing baluster size, the cooling and humidification are increased. Furthermore, a larger baluster has not only more surface area to absorb water vapour and to serve as a surface for evaporation but also more volume, which means that it has more capacity and will therefore release the water for evaporation over a longer period of time.[34]

Obviously the orientation and positioning of the *mashrabīya* relative to the spatial and material organisation of a building and in relation to the environmental exposure is of fundamental importance.

Mashrabīya, al-Suhaymi House, Cairo, Egypt Interior view of a projecting oriel window with wooden Islamic screen wall (*mashrabīya*).

Three principal characteristics of *mashrabīyas* can be summarised as being of central interest for an integrated approach to performance-oriented architecture. Firstly, *mashrabīyas* are multifunctional. Secondly, despite this

multifunctionality, they display a range of aesthetic and formal expressions: different *mashrabīyas* feature floral, abstract Islamic or simple gridded patterns. Thus the entrenched form–function dialectic expires. Thirdly, *mashrabīyas* constitute active boundaries and modulate microclimate. This suggests that the integrated character of *mashrabīyas* fulfils David Leatherbarrow's point of view that:

> a building's performances are the means by which it simultaneously accomplishes practical purposes and gives them legible articulation. Put differently, the appearance and meaning of an architectural work are essentially tied to the operations performed by its several elements. Representational content is not something added to the shaping of settings in response to life's 'bare necessities', as suggested by arguments within the functionalist tradition, but is something intrinsic to the response to those necessities.[35]

In order to pursue this line of argument, research-by-design experiments were carried out by the author and collaborators in different educational contexts so as to examine if screen walls could be developed into a variety of more extensive material systems that could give rise to the notion of an articulated building envelope as an active boundary. In all cases, the research started with material experiments in order to tap into material performance capacity and to operate on characteristic material constraints. The rationale behind the use of material form-finding methods at the beginning of each experiment is to employ the material behaviour in relation to the ranges of stimuli that are expected to act on it. In this way the first two traits of performance-oriented architecture – *material performance* and the *active architectural boundary* – can be addressed in the development of material systems that feature the particular characteristics of screen walls. To increase the potential of multifunctional material systems, such systems could be made non-planar or double-curved to better orientate them in relation to the sun path, prevailing wind directions, etc. This can serve the combined task of microclimatic modulation and spatial provision. The following examples demonstrate such an approach.

Joseph Kellner and David Newton, Proto-Architectures Studio, Rice School of Architecture, Houston, Texas, 2004
The Meta-Patch project by masters students Joseph Kellner and David Newton developed a shape-adaptable plywood screen wall with the multifunctional attributes of *mashrabīyas*.

The ambition of the 'Meta-Patch' project, developed in the 'Proto-Architectures' studio at Rice University, Houston in 2004 by masters students Joseph Kellner and David Newton, was to develop a shape-adaptable plywood screen wall with the multifunctional attributes of the *mashrabīya*. The material system consisted of 51 large rectangular plywood sheets (45 full-size and 6 half-size sheets), onto which 1,920 small

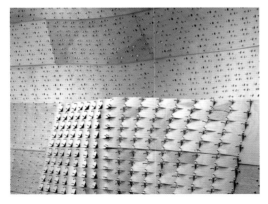

rectangular plywood elements were mounted (40 per full-size large sheet and 20 per half-size large sheet). The small plywood elements were fixed to the larger sheet by means of four bolts, one in each corner. Of these, two in opposing corners were tightly fixed and the other two remained adjustable. On tightening, the adjustable bolts pushed against the larger sheet and forced first the bending of the small elements and then, when tightened further, also the bending of the larger sheet. The curvature of the overall assembly thus derived bottom-up from the cumulative tightening of the 3,600 adjustable bolts. A series of test models with varying patch geometries and material specifications provided the basis for a detailed chart that denoted the correlation of element variables such as size, thickness and fibre orientation, bolt locations and torque settings and the resulting system behaviour. Particular curvature ranges resulting from the full-scale form-finding process enabled the assembly to reach a state of equilibrium, standing by itself and bearing its own weight. In addition the shape of the assembly could perpetually be adapted with the curvature ranges that fulfil multifunctional requirements.

What made the system logic more complex was the addition of functional criteria and related material system features. The large plywood sheets onto which the small elements were mounted were perforated with holes that were covered by the small elements in their flat state. As the bolts were tightened, the perforation was increasingly exposed. In this way both modulation of porosity and adjustment of structural capacity through curvature were correlated with the manipulation of the system's material and geometric behaviour. The orientation of the assembly in relation to environmental conditions, such as the sun path and angle and the wind direction, thus gains similar importance as with the above-discussed Islamic screen walls. However, double curvature enables self-shading or greater exposure to sunlight of areas of the assembly if desired, and within the range of curvature that does not jeopardise the system's structural capacity. Likewise, the size and vector of the opening between the corner of the small element and the hole in the larger sheet modulate pressure and velocity of airflow from one side of the assembly to the other. Visual penetration is equally affected. Each functional criterion may, however, require a different curvature and degree of opening for each region of the assembly, and so the question arises as to how to correlate the interdependent functional attributes of the overall system and its various regions in a controlled way.[36] However, the reliance on manual manipulation draws this experiment in the direction of David Leatherbarrow's aforementioned notion of the 'device paradigm'.[37] Since the intention of the research is not to resort to manual mechanical adjustment, it would be necessary to consider if the material articulation of the system might have the capacity for self-adjustment. The

Typical Norwegian barn, 1950s
This barn was built for the purpose of storing hay. Gaps between the timber planking enable sufficient airflow in order to keep the hay dry and to reduce the impact of wind load on the structure.

examples of the research discussed above in the 'Material Performance' section of this chapter show a possible way forward, in that the hygroscopic behaviour of wood could be employed to shape the assembly. Careful consideration of this aspect in different species of wood, as well as of cut, fibre direction, element geometry and dimensions, and the type of connection between elements, could lead to an assembly that responds to changes in ambient humidity.

A recent survey of a wooden hay barn from the 1950s in Holmsbu, Norway, undertaken by Defne Sunguroğlu Hensel and the author, focused on the envelope of the building. The envelope consists of vertical wooden planks of 150 millimetres in width. Between the planks there are open gaps of about 10 to 15 millimetres that allow for air circulation to dry the hay. In addition these gaps serve to reduce horizontal wind loads on the envelope. The survey focused, among other things, on the interior airflow, and was undertaken during different weather conditions. Of particular interest was the realisation that during a severe snowstorm at temperatures of -10 degrees Celsius plus wind-chill factor, no air movement could be sensed in the interior at a distance of 500 millimetres and more from the envelope, and the felt temperature was considerably warmer than outside. The owner of the barn wishes to convert the building into apartments with the exterior climate envelope coinciding with the envelope of the barn. As a result of the survey, it was proposed instead to set back the climate envelope from the envelope of the barn so as to maintain an intermediary space for adaptive use during different seasons. Such a box-in-box section would result in an extended threshold between interior and exterior and reduce the climate impact on the actual climate envelope. In the case of this intended hay barn conversion, such an approach would enable spaces to be maintained for versatile use during the seasons, as well as being inhabited by other species such as bats

Typical Norwegian barn, 1950s
The interior view of the barn shows the gaps between the planks, as well as the slenderness of the barn's structure.

that could continue to fulfil their important function in the local ecosystem and agricultural pest control.

Recent examples in experimenting with articulated envelopes and associated spatial strategies are promising and feature different types of material systems depending on the context-specific technological infrastructure for production. One striking example is Cloud 9's Media-TIC Building in Barcelona (2010), which employs an assembly of differentiated pneumatic elements and a succinct spatial strategy to increase the interface between interior and exterior. While the Media-TIC building features a meandering vertical space in its sectional articulation, the unbuilt Benetton Headquarters scheme (2009) by studioINTEGRATE features a warped courtyard that opens obliquely to the surroundings with the differentiated pneumatic part of the envelope facing towards the courtyard. Their Saba Naft project (2010), also unbuilt,

Above: Cloud 9, Media-TIC, Barcelona, Spain, 2010
View of the MediaTic showing the layered envelope of the building

Opposite and overleaf: Cloud 9, Media-TIC, Barcelona, Spain, 2010
The Media-TIC building features an assembly of different pneumatic elements combined with a succinct spatial strategy for increasing the interface between interior and exterior.

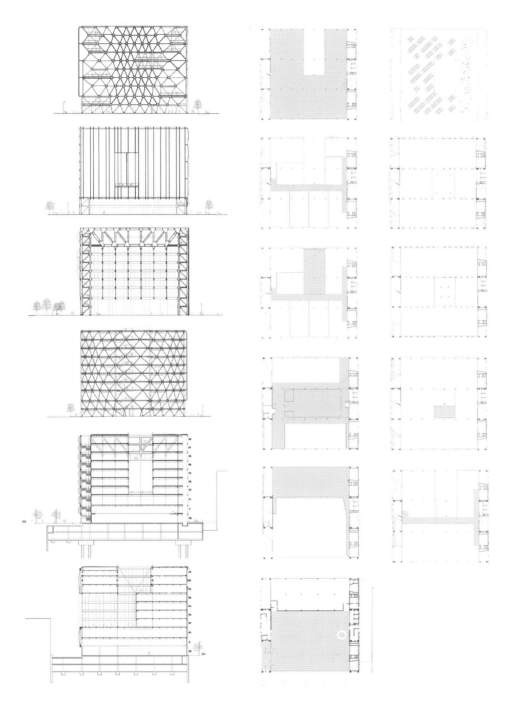

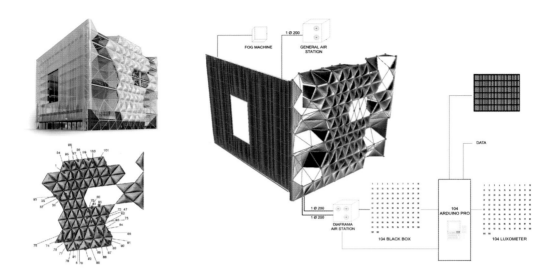

features a similar yet more opened-up scheme. Perhaps one limitation of these otherwise highly promising schemes is that while the particular local climatic context is addressed, the surrounding landscape or buildings are not. However, since the Media-TIC, for instance, is one of the first buildings of an entire masterplan in the process of implementation, it was not possible to address an architectural context that was not in existence during the design phase. This points to the fact that some effort needs to be invested in figuring out how to deal with the unknown in such a design process, since future building activity might affect or perhaps even make redundant the performative capacity of the articulated envelope by changing key contextual aspects such as the local climate and microclimate. At any rate, projects such as these provide useful examples of spatial organisation that can be further informed by other traits of performance-oriented architecture.

Cloud 9, Media-TIC, Barcelona, Spain, 2010.

The Extended Threshold

Having considered the notion of the active architectural boundary and articulated envelope as generators of heterogeneous microclimate, the next step is the spatial organisation and layering of multiple envelopes. The multiplication of envelopes with different kinds and degrees of permeability can serve to articulate sequenced transitions from exterior to interior and vary degrees of non-/discreteness. Envelopes can therefore once again be spatial devices. Architectural history is rich with examples of utilising transitional zones between exterior and interior. Such spaces have largely disappeared and, instead, been replaced by the flat and spatially featureless envelope of the age of power-operated and mechanical-electrically climate-controlled architectures. The former was thus deemed aesthetically old-fashioned and indicative of a time of no comfort; in short it was denounced as a return to some kind of dark medieval slum.

In a research-related meeting in the year 2000, Andrew Hall, at the time director of Arup Facades, pointed out two directions of future research and development of building envelopes. Hall termed the first approach the 'engineer's approach', which focuses on the development of a thin material envelope that is multifunctional and takes care of all the environmental requirements of the building. The second approach Hall termed 'the architect's approach', which focuses on utilising multiple material layers with inhabitable spaces located between them. While evidently the first approach prevails, it would be incorrect to exclusively attribute this fact to the constraints of current standards, expectations or affordability. This

studioINTEGRATE, Benetton Headquarters Competition Entry, Tehran, Iran, 2009
The unbuilt Benetton Headquarters scheme also features a differentiated envelope and a succinct spatial strategy for increasing the interface between interior and exterior. The geometrically highly articulated surface towards the warped courtyard generates a heterogeneous field of effects and microclimates.

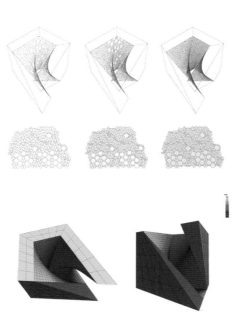

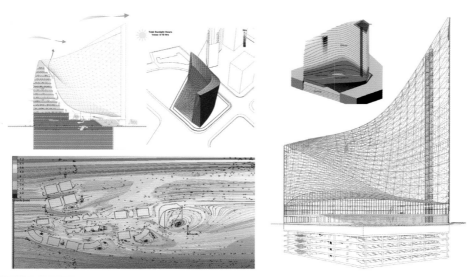

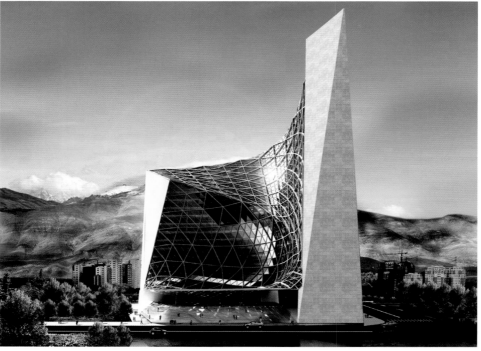

studioINTEGRATE in
collaboration with Dr
Nasrine Faghih and
Archen Consultancy, Saba
Naft Project, Tehran, Iran,
2010
Like the Benetton
Headquarters scheme, the
unbuilt Saba Naft project
features two distinct
articulations of the building
envelope, a more straight-
lined opaque and framing
one, and a curvilinear
and geometrically highly
articulated one. However,
while the Benetton scheme
is more introverted, the
Saba Naft project is explicitly
extrovert.

assessment would not reflect the situation accurately enough. The fact is that a fully developed alternative is not readily at hand; yet a solution could arise from reconceptualisation of the material and spatial boundary.

A great wealth of transitional spaces from throughout architectural history serve as points of reference, and their performative capacity needs to be analysed in order to be modified and used for the purpose at hand. The arcaded space of the Italian Renaissance, for instance, offers such an opportunity for reconceptualisation. Sophia and Stefan Behling described this type of space as 'the wall becoming habitable shade'.[38] This statement emphasises the capacity of such spaces to modulate microclimate, much like the above-discussed Islamic screen walls, but through spatial organisation on the scale of inhabitable space.

David Leatherbarrow discussed different variants of louvre walls by modernist architects, arguing that this building element is of great potential for performative architecture.[39] Leatherbarrow foregrounded the role of orientation, stating that 'because buildings occupy sites, they must "find their bearings" with respect to their environment. Because they accommodate uses, they must cover their volumes with suitable surfaces.'[40] Alan Colquhoun posited that the sun breaker, an external louvred wall, 'was more than a technical device; it introduced a new architectural element in the form of a thick permeable wall'.[41] It is the interaction between this type of building element and the specific environment that it is set within that Leatherbarrow calls 'productive, because its settings supply what the given location is unable to supply on its own',[42] and, moreover:

> Certainly the building's elements are passive – they do not move or change position – but they can also be seen to be active if their 'behaviour' is seen to result in the creation of qualities the world lacks. This is to say, architectural elements are *passively active*. Seemingly at rest, they are secretly at work. The key is this: in their labour, architectural elements fuse themselves into the latencies of the ambient environment, adopting their capacity for change or movement.[43]

Leatherbarrow continued by arguing that modern architecture did not eradicate the architectural boundary as a separation between inside and outside, but instead made this separation subtler as 'boundaries between spatial interiors and exteriors are not overcome with the adoption of the structural frame, but thickened', referring in particular to the louvred wall.[44]

However, the provision of a 'thickened' space as an integral part of the envelope in modernist architectures was not always intended for actual habitation. The work of the second-generation German modernist architect Egon Eiermann, for instance, is characterised by an extensive use of exterior 'wrap-around galleries'.[45] These are elements that do not fulfil the purpose of inhabitation, but instead allow for the maintenance and cleaning of the exterior, as well as structural support and spatial distribution of elements for passive environmental modulation, such as shading. These spaces constitute according to Friederike Hoebel 'constructive and tectonic elements of the three-dimensional façade'.[46] It is interesting to note that Eiermann advocated that 'one should always be careful to examine whether in our climate it is really worth installing so-called air-conditioning, or whether one could achieve equally good results by making special provisions in the construction and using simple ventilation systems'.[47]

The inherent potential of the 'three-dimensional façade' lies therefore in its passive environmental modulation capacity. This realisation can be adopted in the design of contemporary 'thickened' or extended threshold conditions arising from layered envelopes. Moreover, this approach can be applied to existing buildings that can be retrofitted with such layers (see the section later in this chapter on 'Second-Degree Auxiliarity: Supplementary Architectures').

Between 1999 and 2003, Diploma Unit 4 at the Architectural Association in London undertook extensive research-by-design efforts into the extended

Left and opposite: Nasrin Kalbasi and Dimitrios Tsigos, Copenhagen Playhouse Competition Entry, Diploma Unit 4, Architectural Association, London, UK, 2001
Nasrin Kalbasi and Dimitrios Tsigos's Copenhagen Playhouse scheme features a striated tectonic that defines the envelope as a permeable enclosure and provides an extended threshold and continuous space between the exterior and interior landscape of the project along multiple routes through the site.

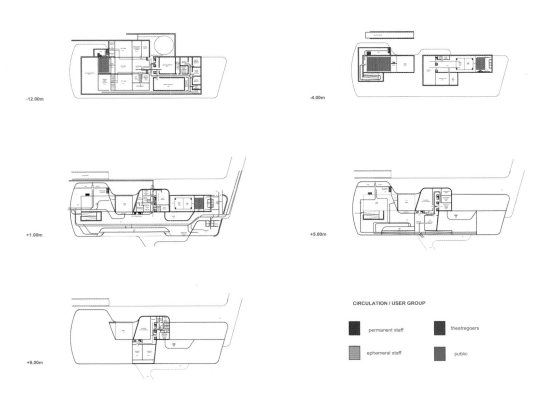

-12.00m

-4.00m

+1.00m

+5.00m

+9.00m

CIRCULATION / USER GROUP

permanent staff

theatregoers

ephemeral staff

public

threshold. These aimed at the synthesis between non-discrete architecture and inhabitable boundary applied to the design of entire buildings. Examples include the scheme for the Copenhagen Playhouse competition by Nasrin Kalbasi and Dimitrios Tsigos and the Temporal House design by Hani Fallaha and Dimitrios Tsigos. In both cases the entire envelope is articulated as a type of louvre wall extended into a 'striated' tectonic, a notion inspired by the works of the Finnish sculptor Raimo Utriainen (1927–1994) and developed by the Iranian architect Bahram Shirdel. In the case of the Copenhagen Playhouse scheme, the striated tectonic defines the envelope as both a permeable enclosure and an inhabitable continuous exterior and interior landscape. The size range, geometric articulation of and transition between the elements that make up the striated envelope and landscape surface of the project all change in relation to their primary purpose as a space-defining element or as a furnishing surface scaled to accommodate the

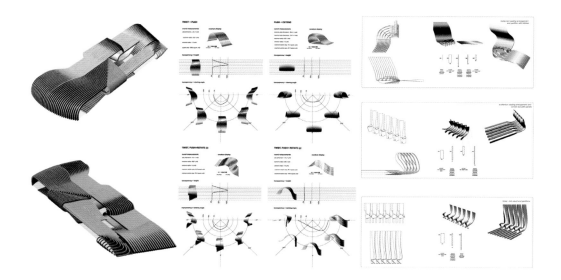

human body. Thus the monumental scale flows in a continuous movement to the scale of the human body and vice versa. The Temporal House design pursued a similar strategy but reduced the size range of the striated tectonic as it operates in much closer proximity to the human body. Pneumatic cushions between the striated elements provide adaptable enclosure and surface for appropriation.

OCEAN Design Research Association's scheme for the unbuilt Frankfurter Strasse Apartment Block in Cologne, Germany (1998) replaced space use allocation (living room, kitchen, bedroom etc) with spaces that provide different microclimates, delivering an element of choice and adaptive use to the residents. The project features three different envelopes – transparent, veiling (screen wall) and opaque – that feature variation in the distance between the layers and the order of their layering. Each combination results in a unique range of conditions per room. As no references or standards existed for such a design, the local authorities did not grant planning permission.

A more recent example is the diploma project by Joakim Hoen undertaken in late 2011 at the Oslo School of Architecture and Design. The core aim of the project was to develop design strategies and computational methods

Nasrin Kalbasi and Dimitrios Tsigos, Copenhagen Playhouse Competition Entry, Diploma Unit 4, Architectural Association, London, UK, 2001
The Copenhagen Playhouse scheme features size ranges and transition of the striated envelope and landscape surface of the project, changing smoothly from space-defining to envelope- and surface-articulating to furnishing elements.

Opposite: Hani Fallaha and Dimitrios Tsigos, Experimental House, Diploma Unit 4, Architectural Association, London, UK, 2002–3.

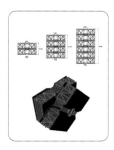
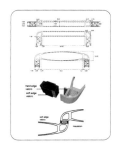
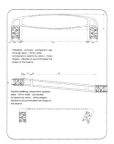

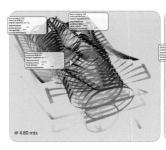
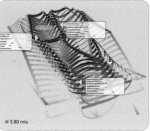
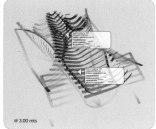

@ 4.80 mts

@ 3.80 mts

@ 3.00 mts

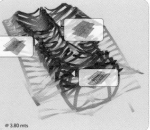
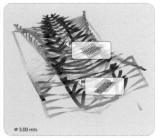

@ 4.80 mts

@ 3.80 mts

@ 3.00 mts

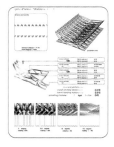
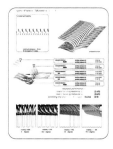
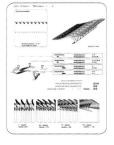
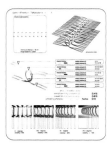

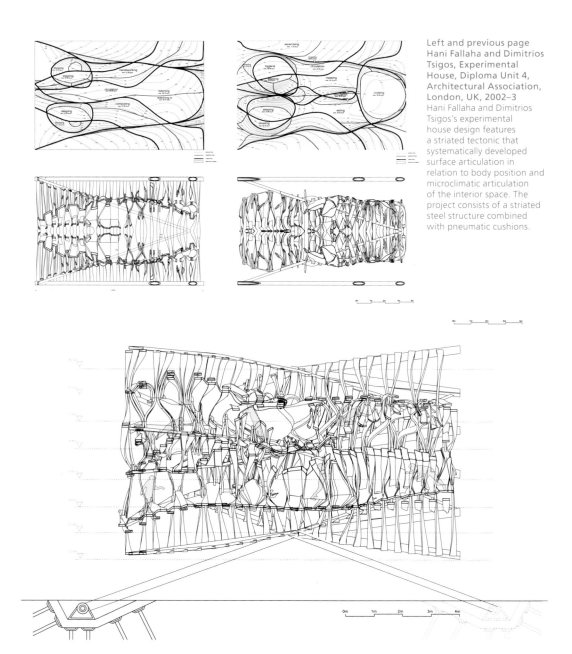

Left and previous page
Hani Fallaha and Dimitrios
Tsigos, Experimental
House, Diploma Unit 4,
Architectural Association,
London, UK, 2002–3
*Hani Fallaha and Dimitrios
Tsigos's experimental
house design features
a striated tectonic that
systematically developed
surface articulation in
relation to body position and
microclimatic articulation
of the interior space. The
project consists of a striated
steel structure combined
with pneumatic cushions.*

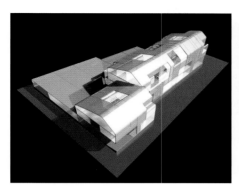

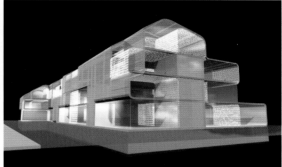

OCEAN, Frankfurter
Strasse Apartment Block,
Cologne, Germany, 1998
OCEAN's design study for
an unexecuted apartment
block in Cologne articulates
envelope and spaces
concurrently by varying
the position and distances
between opaque, veiling and
transparent material layers.
This strategy results in living
units with heterogeneous
interior climates that provide
choices for different modes
and patterns of inhabitation
and space use.

for a multiple-envelope non-standard coastal holiday home for southern Norway. The specific terrain and the severe coastal wind and weather conditions served as environmental input into the design process and informed the articulation of the outer screen-type envelope. The scheme interiorises the context-specific landscape experience and integrates provisions into the inner envelope, such as the work surface of the kitchen and the alcoves for the bedsides. The articulation of the outer screen-like envelope concerned primarily the dissipation of horizontal wind loads and reduction of climate impact on the inner envelope, as well as the deceleration of airflow velocity from the exterior to the intermediary space to make it useable even during more severe weather conditions.

It is helpful also to recognise the built environment as a vast repository of historical knowledge. With this in mind, the Sustainable Environment Association (SEA) was founded in Norway in 2011 to examine architectural history from a performance perspective. A number of projects are being analysed with particular regard to gradual transitions between exterior and interior and the production of heterogeneous microclimate.[48] One of these is the Baghdad Kiosk, a small two-storey structure dating from 1638–9 that is located in the Fourth Courtyard of Istanbul's Topkapı Palace. Defne Sunguroğlu Hensel has studied the spatial organisation and environmental performance of this Ottoman building, which was mainly used as a summer or winter recreational residence.[49] It is organised on an octagonal footprint with four of the faces recessed, resulting in a meandering envelope thickened by an arcaded space. This particular spatial and material organisation results

in different exterior spaces that are set back and shaded by the protruding roof. It also positions the windows in the protruding corners in a more exposed part of the envelope to gain light for the interior. Moreover, it results in areas of different climatic exposure in the interior, which it organises into four apses that are occupied by divans. These provide diverse choices of locations for specific activities relative to the time-specific preferences of the inhabitants that 'adapt' by relocating. In addition, the arcades could either be fully exposed or covered by hanging carpets and textile draping, transforming the upper level into exposed or private zones. Textile draping can provide visual protection, shading and ventilation. What is surprising is the ratio between the transitional arcaded space and the interior space, which are equal in area. Clearly the transitional space was deemed neither wasteful nor secondary, but instead an essential provision for versatile use.

Spatial transitions that generate heterogeneous microclimate can also benefit the purpose of species integration of architecture. Species integration in architecture might evolve out of the combined study of three areas: the ecological niche of a species; conditions characteristic of animal-made shelters; and shelters for different species made by humans. The first and second types of study are typical for biologists but entirely foreign to architects. In order to bring architects up to task, educational measures need to be taken. Here it is useful to focus on the third type of study: human-made shelters for different

Joakim Hoen, Diploma Project, Oslo School of Architecture and Design, Norway, 2011
Joakim Hoen focused on the development of design strategies and methods for multiple-envelope non-standard coastal holiday homes for southern Norway. The computational design process for the outer envelopes is informed by local climate and terrain data, while the inner envelope is informed by integration of provisions and terrain data.

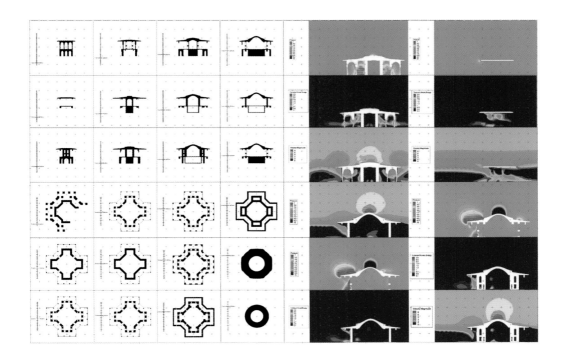

Above: Baghdad Kiosk, Topkapı Palace, Istanbul, Turkey, 1638–9
This analysis focused on the combined spatial and material articulation and environmental performance analysis of the Baghdad Kiosk.
Left: Vertical and horizontal sectional sequences indicating the intricate articulation and variation of the combined spatial and material deep threshold of the kiosk.
Right: Computational fluid dynamics (CFD) analysis of airflow velocities, pressure zones and turbulent kinetic energy, indicating the environmental effects and interaction of the kiosk.

species. There are many interesting historical examples of architectures designed to house different animal species that might indicate potentials for contemporary architectures. The following paragraphs focus on pigeon towers and dovecotes as a particularly diverse range of context-specific provisions.

During the Safavid period (1501–1722) of the Persian Empire, a noteworthy special-purpose building type flourished in the Isfahan region: the pigeon tower. The purpose of these buildings, which were up to 20 metres in height, was to provide shelter for pigeons and to collect the pigeon dung as fertiliser for agriculture, in particular for growing melons, as well as for use in Isfahan's tanneries for softening of leather.[50] Circular or rectangular in plan with internally buttressed walls, pigeon towers could either be freestanding single structures, or be integrated into the outer walls of gardens. Larger towers could house over 10,000 pigeons. Such towers consisted either of a single hollow space or drum or of an inner drum enclosed by an outer one. Some towers were organised as eight connected drums around a central one, thus increasing the surface area of the interior and hence the number of pigeonholes. Atop the towers, turrets with honeycomb brickwork provided entry and exit for the pigeons. Humans normally accessed the tower only once a year to harvest the dung.[51] As the analysis undertaken by the Sustainable Environment Association shows, the immense thermal mass of these structures in combination with their effective natural ventilation resulted in an 'interior' climate that seemed to appeal to wild pigeons.

Structures for the same use can be found in Anatolia: the large rectangular dovecotes (*boranhane*) in the Diyarbakir region[52] and the often densely clustered half-above- and half-below-ground ones built on the steep slopes in the Kayseri region. The latter are characterised by a stone-made above-ground tower-like part (*burç*) that is rectangular, square, circular or elliptical in plan and provides access for the pigeons, and a cave-like rock-hewn underground part (*kuşhane*) that accommodates the nests. A short tunnel and a door from the lower part of the slope provided human access for harvesting the dung.[53] These half-underground structures are sheltered from the severe Anatolian winter conditions; this protection, presumably coupled with the body temperature of the pigeons, maintains a suitable 'interior' environment.

Pigeon Tower, Isfahan, Iran, *c* 1650
Left: Sectional axonometric view.
Centre: The transient thermal analysis shows that the thermal mass of the adobe wall buffers daily temperature fluctuations effectively. (Sponsored by RadTherm®)
by RadTherm
Right: The computational fluid dynamics (CFD) analysis of airflow shows effective wind-driven ventilation throughout the structure. (Temporary licences sponsored by EnSight®)

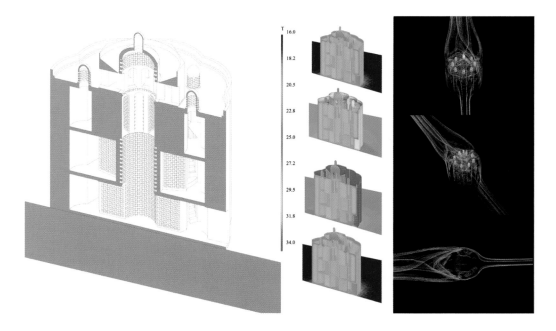

The Roman Empire has its equivalent in the dovecote (*columbarium*). It is assumed that the Romans introduced dovecotes throughout their Empire. In the course of time dovecotes emerged throughout medieval Europe and took different shapes in Italy, France, the United Kingdom, throughout Eastern Europe and eventually in North America. Of especial interest are dovecotes that are not freestanding structures, but instead integrated into other buildings. In particular in the United Kingdom, dovecotes were often integrated in the gable walls of barns and sometimes farmhouses. In general the integration of livestock in the same building as humans has been known throughout the ages in agricultural societies, serving purposes of both safety and heat gain from the bodies of the animals. The purpose of rethinking this option today would be to initiate a non-anthropocentric architecture that utilises an extended threshold to sustain biodiversity.

Second-Degree Auxiliarity: Supplementary Architectures

An important question arises from the previous section of this chapter: is the notion of the extended threshold only of use for newly designed architectures, or does it bear any relevance for the bulk of already existing ones that cannot simply be taken down and replaced? What can be done with buildings, even entire quarters or settlements, that can still accommodate decades of use during which only the facades or the interior may be renewed a few times? Works like the venerated Church of the Holy Sepulchre in the Old City of Jerusalem, which was built in stages as new constructions around existing ones, suggest a surprising possibility: it is indeed possible to build layers of envelopes and spaces outwards from an existing core. The picture that emerges suggests an entire new market segment to architecture and the industries involved in the making of the built environment: supplementary layers of material systems or what are here referred to as *second-degree auxiliary* architectures around existing architectures.

Architectural history is rich with such supplementary interventions that can provide varying degrees of shelter. The interest of the German architect Frei Otto and his collaborators at the Institute for Lightweight Structures in Stuttgart in suspended and convertible roofs and light means of providing shelter led to research into historical precedents, culminating in Rainer Graefe's doctoral thesis on the *vela* (sun sails) of Roman theatres and the subsequent publication of a book on the topic.[54] This was followed by the Institute for Lightweight Structures publication *Schattenzelte: Sun and*

Shade – Toldos, Vela,[55] which included research on Spanish *toldos* (awnings) and Roman *vela*, as well as convertible sunroofs in Japan. In particular the latter two are of interest in that these were not part of the initial design of a building. In the aforementioned book, Heribert Hamann and José Luis Moro describe the Spanish *toldo* as follows:

> An architectural feature which has been largely ignored, is the awning (Spanish: 'toldo') which is still extensively used today … Toldos are designed to protect against excessive insolation thereby reducing the heating of the air volume underneath the toldo, protecting the public against air-borne dust and sometimes against glare. Their space-enclosing and space-creating effect is most impressive … .[56]

Hamann and Moro pointed out that two predominant types of *toldos* had evolved: the *cortège toldo* and the *street toldo*. The former consists of 'individual awning segments which are sewn or thonged together' and are 'suspended from masts and cannot be drawn'.[57] The latter is 'suspended at guttering height between opposite rows of houses flanking the shopping streets. The street *toldo* can be extended or drawn using a curtain-type mechanism.'[58] Similar types of awnings are also in use in the Near East and Mediterranean North Africa, parts of Central America and Japan. Berthold Burkhardt described the convertible sunroofs in Japan as follows:

> The Japanese awning consists of ropes which are stretched across the road between houses at a height of ca. 4 metres. If there are no houses on one side of the road the support ropes are fixed to a simple wooden structure.[59]

As these existing examples show, sun sails are typically either freestanding structures, or suspended between buildings or, alternatively, protrude from a building. In addition Fritz Lang described a series of design elaborations that add new systems to the remit of existing ones, including what he termed 'horizontal grid shades', sun shades with stretcher bars, and 'feather shades', all developed in Frei Otto's atelier in Warmbronn.[60]

There are two characteristics of the supplementary architectures portrayed in the book on *Sun and Shade – Toldos, Vela*[61] that are worth examining: firstly, they are mainly in use in warm climates; and secondly, the new designs depicted in the book tend to be repetitive assemblies in which the components, whether sail or grid, are uniform. From this realisation, two interesting questions arise. Can such systems be of use in cold climates? And can the versatility of these supplementary architectures be enhanced by way of non-uniform components that are varied in geometry and size?

Considerable effort has been invested in particular into the development of non-uniform membrane systems, which are form-active tension systems that acquire their optimal structural shape under tension. For example, in the context of the 'Micro-Ecologies' studio at London Metropolitan University in 2006–7, diploma student Kazutaka Fujii developed a system which consisted of layered continuous membranes that were locally cut in a specific pattern and interconnected by way of minimal holes. A three-dimensional metal lattice served as a frame for the membrane layers. Once the system had been developed, the cutting and connection pattern of the layers was iteratively altered and the resulting self-shading pattern and cross-ventilation was measured both on and close to the back and front surfaces of the assembly, as well as at a distance from it. An extensive series of experiments made it possible to reverse the information flow in the experiment and to commence from desired environmental conditions so as to derive the associated articulation of the membrane system. This served as proof that the relation between specific system configurations and related environmental modulation was sufficiently understood. In a subsequent phase the system was further developed into a screen-wall-type envelope for a transitional space at a specific site in Japan that aimed to enable the development of micro-ecologies. However, the digital model of the design was at the time too complex to be subjected to detailed environmental modulation analysis.

In another example, 100 second- and third-year students in architecture participated in the 'Auxiliary Architectures – Membrane and Cable-Net Systems' workshop at the Izmir University of Economics in 2009. Twenty teams of five students each were introduced to form-finding increasingly

Kazutaka Fujii, Micro-Ecologies Studio, London Metropolitan University, UK, 2006–7
The differentiated membrane system developed by Kazutaka Fujii consists of two layers of membranes with minimal holes spanned between three layers of metal grid. The system makes possible a finely graded light and shading modulation.

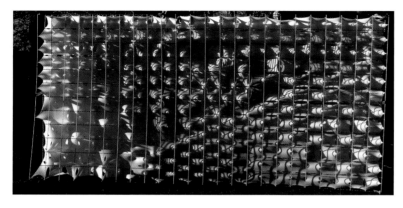

Left: Kazutaka Fujii, Micro-Ecologies Studio, London Metropolitan University, UK, 2006–7
An extensive series of full-scale experiments enabled a detailed understanding of minimal holes orientation and distribution per membrane layer in relation to desired light and shading modulation.

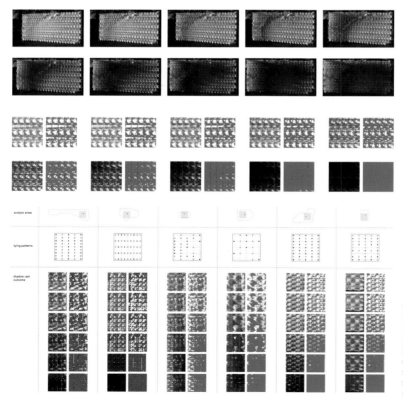

Opposite: Kazutaka Fujii, Micro-Ecologies Studio, London Metropolitan University, UK, 2006–7
In parallel to physical experiments, an extensive series of digital light and shading analyses served to refine the design method in relation to the production of the desired conditions.

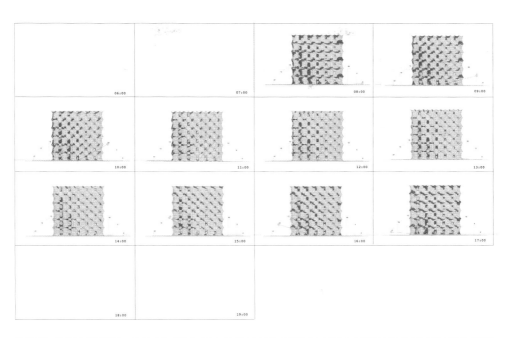

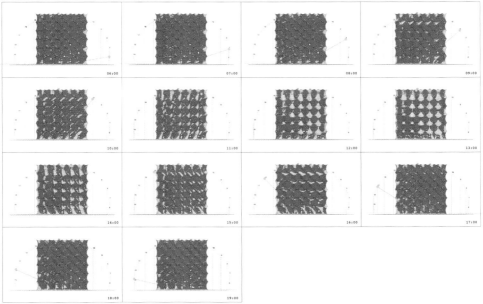

Auxiliary Architectures
– Membrane Spaces
Workshop, Izmir
University of Economics,
Izmir, Turkey, 2009
The 'Auxiliary Architectures
– Membrane Spaces'
workshop at Izmir University
of Economics focused
on the development of
differentiated membrane
and cable-net systems and
their climatic modulation
capacity. A hundred
students participated in this
endeavour.

complex membrane and cable-net systems. Like membranes, cable nets are form-active tension structures that reach their optimal structural shape under tension. These systems and their related form-finding methods were separately pioneered and extensively developed by Frei Otto from the 1950s onwards. However, the combination of the two systems into arrays of non-uniform membranes set within non-uniform cable nets has not been widely explored. The integration of these two systems requires nested multiple-hierarchy form-found systems. One of the issues that need to be considered when designing such systems as supplementary to an existing built environment is the availability of structural anchor points. The collected tensile forces of such a system can be considerable, and lack of structural capacity in the existing buildings to receive such forces might severely limit options for anchorage. This requires the cable net to be designed with the available anchor points as primary constraints.

Typically membrane systems were used for large uninterrupted covers, even if those were made from separate elements. The systems developed in the workshop are, however, in intent associated with the Islamic screen walls discussed above (see the section of this chapter on 'The Active Architectural Boundary, the Articulated Envelope and Heterogeneous Environments'). Depending on their size range, density and orientation to climatic exposure, such membrane arrays can thus be thought of as generating similar microclimatic conditions as does the foliage of trees or tall shrubs. When returning to the constraints imposed by the anchor points, it might seem that there is a risk of a mismatch between the possible form of the cable net and the desired orientation of the individual membranes for optimal environmental modulation. This can, however, be resolved by the introduction of compression members that can help spread the net into the desired spatial configuration to orient the individual membranes in the desired manner. Likewise the individual membranes can be altered in shape or divided into smaller patches that are oriented with the help of secondary cable nets that are nested within the primary net, as well as additional compression members. As the systems gain a high level of articulation, it is necessary to frequently revisit the different levels of hierarchy in the system to check whether the present logic can be retained or whether it needs to be altered due to changes that trigger system adaptations upwards and downwards in scale in the form-finding process.

As the overall system develops, it is also necessary to undertake at each step an analysis of the environmental conditions produced by the system in a location- and time-specific manner. In the workshop, the resulting shading

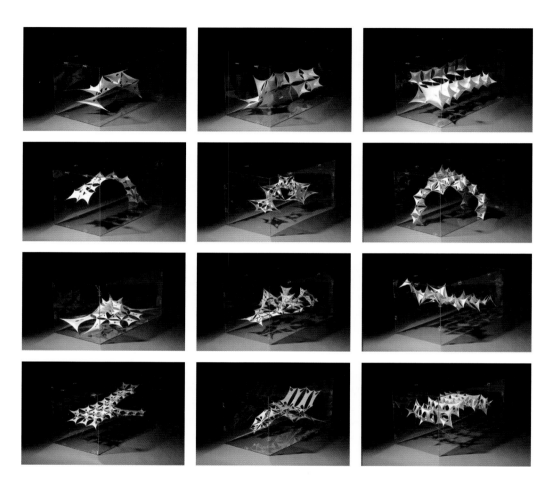

and self-shading capacity was analysed both with physical models and by way of computational modelling and analysis. This iterative process of system development through complex form-finding operations enables the analysis of the conditions produced by the system in each particular configuration.

During the 12-day workshop, 20 different membrane and cable-net systems were developed. The defining characteristics were compared in the process, differences were enhanced and a method of classification for the various systems was established. Continuous spatial nets, branching spatial nets and self-supporting tensegrity systems were developed, each with varying mesh

Auxiliary Architectures
– Membrane Spaces
Workshop, Izmir
University of Economics,
Izmir, Turkey, 2009
Twelve of the 20 different
membrane and cable-net
systems developed in the
workshop.

102

sizes. Membranes were tested as triangular patches in hexagonal arrays, as hyperbolic paraboloids, hyperboloids or cones. Membranes were connected to each other or to cable nets at their corners between their surfaces, as well as by means of minimal holes. Compression elements and bending rods were tested to rearticulate the systems spatially.

The final task of the workshop was the full-scale construction of one of the systems on the premises of the university to demonstrate the spatial and environmental modulation capacity of such a differentiated system in interaction with the environment. A specific design was developed for an uninteresting corridor space. Since the corridor was glazed and facing the exterior on its long sides, it was possible to implement the aim for environmental modulation in the interior. During the morning hours the system operates as a shading screen that at the same time maintains views towards the exterior. At sunset the light of the low-angle sun is reflected back into the corridor and is thus amplified. This revealed the unanticipated opportunity to consider a screen-wall-type system that typically faces the exterior on one side only, as a system exposed to environmental input from both sides.

OCEAN's Bylgja project at the FRAC Centre in Orléans (2008) also consisted of a branching cable-net and membrane array combination, while their

Auxiliary Architectures – Membrane Spaces Workshop, Izmir University of Economics, Izmir, Turkey, 2009
A full-scale differentiated membrane and cable-net system developed in the workshop. The system amplifies the low-angle sunlight in the evening in the dark corridor space.

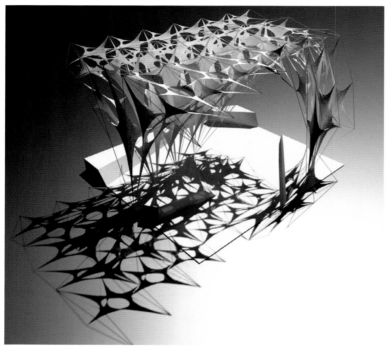

OCEAN, MM-Tent
Membrella, 2008
The MM-Tent Membrella
project consists of a
freestanding membrane
and strut system that
can be added to existing
architectures so as to
organise space and provide
heterogeneous climatic
modulation.

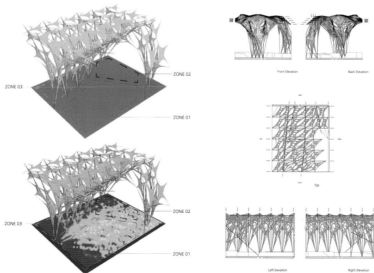

OCEAN, Bylgja
Membrane and Cable-
Net Installation, FRAC
– Le Fonds régional d'art
contemporain, Orléans,
France, 2008
The Bylgja installation
consisted of a branching
cable net that supported an
array of 60 differentiated
membranes which were
used to modulate the light
conditions in the exhibition
space.

MM-Tent Membrella project (2008) constitutes a freestanding version of this type of system. Likewise the membrane project at OCEAN's Open City in Ritoque in Chile – developed in the context of the 'Scarcity and Creativity in Latitude 33' studio and the Research Center for Architecture and Tectonics at the Oslo School of Architecture and Design – is structurally self-stabile and designed to withstand the often severe Pacific coastal winds.

OCEAN's M-Velope project (2012) constitutes both a differentiated screen and an extended threshold between the interior of the Cooper Union building in New York City and the exterior street space. M-Velope consists of a steel mesh of varying porosity and an array of membranes that together modulate the luminous and sonic environment and provide a layered heterogeneous space. The design was elaborated additionally by considerations of specific views and sightlines from the street to the screened space and vice versa, not unlike Islamic screen walls.

These projects show that differentiated membrane systems can generate finely nuanced heterogeneous spatial and environmental conditions specific to each context, configuration and orientation. Differentiated membrane systems are of interest in that they can share some properties of foliage of complex vegetation systems regarding

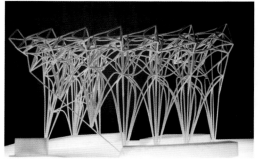

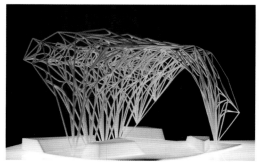
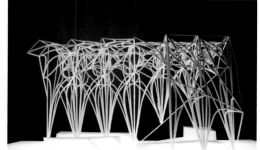

the production of microclimate. As Tim Oke wrote:

> The three-dimensional geometr[ies] of a leaf or a canopy layer … are
> particularly interesting because they have both upper and lower active
> surfaces. This greatly increases their effective surface area for radiative
> and convective exchange … On a plant or tree the leaf is not in
> isolation, it is intimately linked to its total environmental setting, and the same
> is true of a plant or tree in a crop or forest. The effects of multiple shading,
> multiple reflection, long-wave radiation interaction etc. provide important
> feedbacks not found in the isolated case.[62]

The level of complexity that is involved confronts microclimatologists
with considerable difficulties in analysing and modelling the microclimatic
conditions produced by complex vegetation systems. Oke pointed out that

> faced with such a system it might perhaps seem appropriate to analyse the
> climate of a typical leaf and then to integrate this over the number of leaves
> to give the climate of the plant or tree, and then to integrate those climates to

OCEAN, MM-Tent
Membrella, 2008
The MM-Tent Membrella
project consists of a
freestanding membrane
and strut system that
can be added to existing
architectures so as to
organise space and provide
heterogeneous climatic
modulation.

Las Piedras del Cielo –
Membrane Shelter – Open
City Ritoque, Scarcity
and Creativity in Latitude
33 Master-Studio, Oslo
School of Architecture
and Design, Norway, 2012
The membrane shelter
designed by masters
students at the Oslo
School of Architecture and
Design for the Open City
in Ritoque in Chile consists
of a landform podium with
embedded spaces and a
roof of nine membranes.
The structure will serve as a
sheltered meeting, cooking
and eating area for the Open
City.

arrive at the climate of a crop or forest. Unfortunately it is not possible to make
… a linear extrapolation of elemental units and thereby to combine many
microclimates into a local climate.[63]

Nevertheless this indicates that it may be of interest for architects who design
differentiated membrane systems to collaborate with microclimatologists who
analyse foliage systems.

Second-degree auxiliary architectures need not exclusively focus on
lightweight designs. Any of the systems portrayed in the previous sections
of this chapter can equally be designed as a supplementary architecture.
The selection of a system or combination of systems requires context-
specific performance criteria. In the context of the 'Auxiliary Architectures'
studio at the Oslo School of Architecture and Design, Rikard Jaucis and
Joakim Hoen's 2010 scheme for a new security perimeter for the Eero
Saarinen-designed American Embassy in Oslo combines perimeter parking
with a sculptural steel-plate screen that affects nuanced light modulation in
the area adjacent to the perimeter. Off-the-shelf structural analysis software

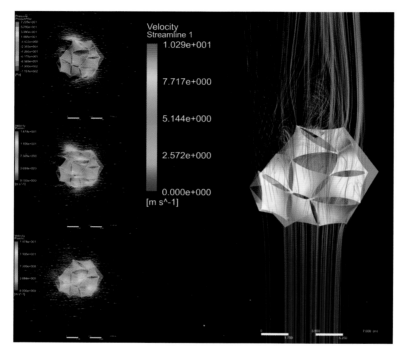

Velocity
Streamline 1

1.029e+001

7.717e+000

5.144e+000

2.572e+000

0.000e+000
[m s^-1]

Las Piedras del Cielo –
Membrane Shelter – Open
City Ritoque, Scarcity
and Creativity in Latitude
33 Master-Studio, Oslo
School of Architecture
and Design, Norway, 2012
The membrane shelter must
be capable of withstanding
the typically high wind
loads of the Pacific coastal
areas in the region.
Articulating the shelter not
as a continuous membrane
roof, but instead as a more
open configuration of nine
membranes, helps to reduce
pressure gradients and uplift.
It is important, however,
to analyse the resulting
airflow conditions within and
around the shelter in order
to prevent acceleration of
airflow beyond acceptable
limits. (Temporary licences
sponsored by EnSight®)

was repurposed to form-find the scored steel plates based on their
deformation under force. The resulting double curvature of the steel plates
is developed in relation to time- and season-specific sun angles in order to
prevent or enable views towards the embassy.

As the above shows, the production of heterogeneous microclimates
of differentiated supplementary architectures can entail a high level of
complexity for one system. As soon as several systems are combined
and interact, the complexity increases further. The difficulties involved in
developing such systems and associated design methods are, however,
not insurmountable. The research undertaken with students who had
no prior experience in this way of working showed that it was possible
to reach an elevated level of control of the system definition and
environmental modulation in a relatively short time. For more complex
systems it is necessary to develop, in addition to the material experiments,
computational methods to facilitate feedback between system articulation
and environmental performance. The development of such methods is

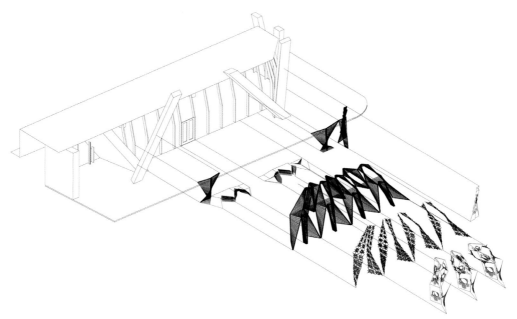

currently under way in many educational and research contexts around the world, but such efforts require systematic conceptual underpinning.

First-Degree Auxiliarity: Embedded Architectures

Although constructions constitute finite operations in terms of their material extent, they can be *embedded* into numerous larger systems and engage in complex processes. Three key notions are related to this concept: context-specificity, auxiliarity and non-discreteness. The late Hassan Fathy argued that architectural 'form has meaning only within the context of its environment'.[64] For Fathy, this entailed the close interrelation of specific local knowledge and skills in construction, local climate, locally available materials, and so on. Pietro Laureano – architect, urban planner and UNESCO consultant for arid regions, water management, Islamic civilisation and endangered ecosystems – extended this view by positing that 'each traditional practice is not an expedient to solve a single problem, but it is an elaborated and often a multipurpose system that is part of an integral approach (society, culture and economy) which is strictly linked to an idea of the world based on the careful management of local resources.'[65]

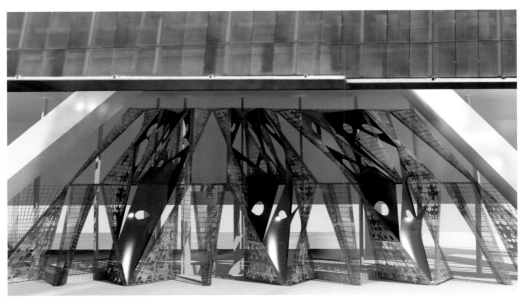

OCEAN, M-Velope Phase 1, 2012
OCEAN's M-Velope project constitutes both a differentiated screen and an extended threshold.

Opposite: Joakim Hoen and Rikard Jaucis, Auxiliary Architectures Studio, Oslo School of Architecture and Design, 2010
Top: Axonometric of the proposed perimeter structure for the American embassy in Oslo.
Centre: Sunlight reflection and shading pattern of differently curved and scored steel panels. Bottom: Sunlight reflection and shading pattern in the context of the site.

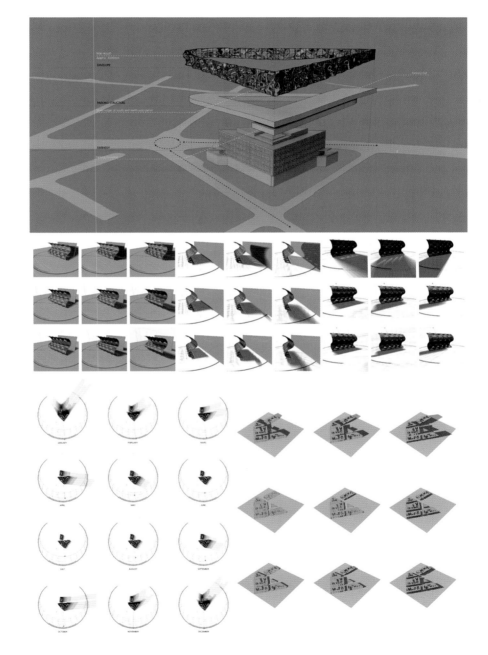

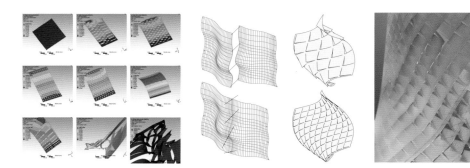

Moreover, Frei Otto described an obvious, yet fundamentally important and often overlooked trait of architecture when he stated that 'constructions are auxiliary means, not an end in themselves.'[66] As an example, Otto specified that a bridge is auxiliary to the road system of which it is part. In this particular case *auxiliarity* is related to the primary function of the bridge in relation to a single larger system, namely the road network. However, architectures can be simultaneously auxiliary to several systems and this can include conditions that are not man-made. As already mentioned (see chapter 3), David Leatherbarrow argued that architecture always 'participates in numerous authored and un-authored conditions'.[67] The latter includes, for instance, the interaction of constructions with local climate and the resulting production of microclimate, as well as the interaction of architectures with cultural patterns (of use) and the coupling of these two conditions. This implies that if 'participation' and its consequences are not considered, the resulting conditions will be accidental. The difference between Otto's notion of *auxiliarity* and Leatherbarrow's notion of *participation* rests therefore in the fact that the former entails intentional functional relations, while the latter takes place whether considered by the architect or not.

The extent to which an architecture is auxiliary to other conditions and the quality of its participation can be made a central concern of an architectural design and thus emphasise embeddedness, auxiliarity and participation. It is therefore interesting to examine cases that are intricately embedded in numerous systems across scales and that participate at the same time in local circumstances and produce desirable conditions and effects. This type of auxiliary relation is referred to here as *first-degree auxiliarity* or *embedded architecture*.

Architectural history is rich in embedded architectures that are auxiliary to man-made and natural systems at many different scales. One noteworthy

Joakim Hoen and Rikard Jaucis, Auxiliary Architectures Studio, Oslo School of Architecture and Design, Norway, 2010
Joakim Hoen and Rikard Jaucis repurposed an off-the-shelf structural-analysis software package for computational form-finding.
Left: Deformation of scored steel panels under tension and bending.
Centre: Double-curved steel panel geometry.
Right: Physical prototype.

example is the Khaju Bridge (*pol-e khajoo*), built around AD 1650 under the Safavid Shah Abbas II on the foundations of an older bridge spanning across the Zayandeh River in Isfahan, Iran. Isfahan is located at an altitude of 1,590 metres, and the Köppen climate classification designates its climate a cold desert. Summers are hot, average winter days are mild and winter nights can be cold. At 132 metres long and 14 metres wide, the two-storey masonry Khaju Bridge features a 7.5-metre-wide roadway on its upper storey that is framed on both sides by arched spaces, while the lower storey comprises a vaulted space that can only be reached by pedestrians. The bridge weir combines 18 low-flow deep channels equipped with sluice gates and stepped cascades for large flood flows, which serve to dissipate hydraulic energy.[68] The sluice gates serve to regulate the water level of the Zayandeh River for the purpose of irrigation of upstream gardens etc. Yet the bridge's fulfilment of its primary functions regarding the urban circulation system and water management is only part of its auxiliarity to larger systems. The stepped chutes on its downstream side double up as seating for public use. Here, as well as in the tier of arches and vaulted space of the lower storey, evaporative cooling and airflow generate a comfortable microclimate during the hot months of the year. From this perspective the spatial and material organisation of the bridge is inherently multifunctional. It thus combines a civic project with the provision of a climatically comfortable public space for appropriation and social assembly.[69]

First-degree auxiliarity is clearly not an exclusive attribute of representational architectures (theatres, palaces etc) or of civic architectures. Pre-industrial vernacular architectures also provide abundant examples. In his report to the United Nations Convention to Combat Desertification, Laureano described various historical and regionally specific settlement types in the dry areas of the Mediterranean with particular focus on their characteristic interrelation between water management, the associated facilitation of agriculture and local economy, and the nuanced modulation of spaces for habitation.[70] Furthermore, Laureano pointed out that these settlements and architectures had a critical role in the production and maintenance of the cultural landscape they were set within. He referred to one of the core modes of generating suitable conditions as the 'oasis effect':

> a *virtuous cycle* is established which can run itself and regenerate itself. This
> process can be used as a pattern that can be applied for all the situations,
> also for non-desert lands, whereby islands of fertility are created and is
> defined as follows: 'an oasis is a human settlement in a harsh geographical

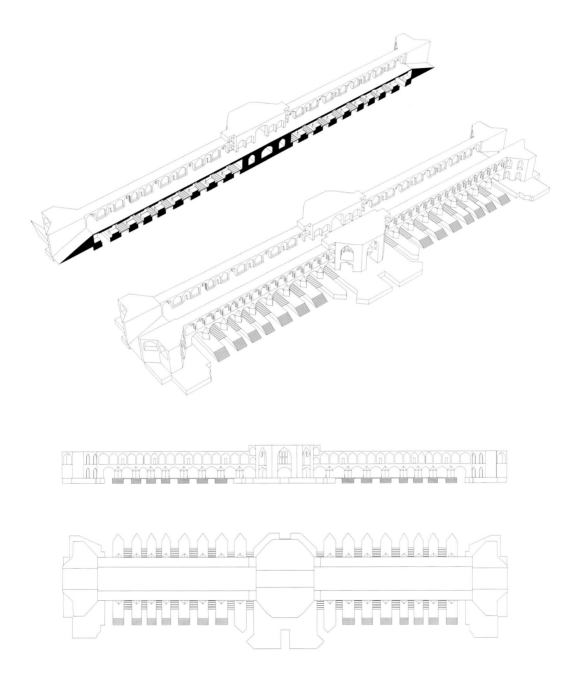

Left: Khaju Bridge (*pol-e khajoo*), Isfahan, Iran, *c* 1650
Axonometric section, axonometric, elevation and plan of the Kahju Bridge.

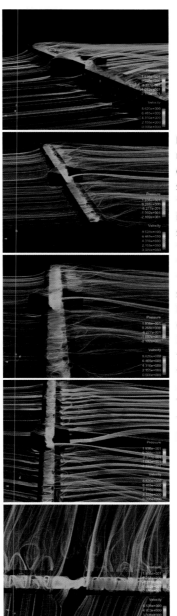

situation that uses rare resources which are available locally in order to spark off a rising amplification of positive interactions and create a fertile, self-sustaining environmental niche which is in direct contrast with the unfavourable surroundings'.[71]

Laureano went on to describe the 'oasis model' in 'urban ecosystems' such as caravan-route towns that arise from sophisticated irrigation systems which utilise 'favourable geomorphological situations in geographic systems'.[72] Moreover, he showed how the socio-cultural groups of 'hunter-gatherers', 'farmer-breeders' and 'agro-pastoralists', as well as 'oasis' and 'urban ecosystem' groupings, utilise their specific environmental systems differently. In extending this thought, he examined different types of systems of traditional knowledge use for water management to sustain settlements and agriculture in the arid areas of the Mediterranean that undergo desertification and degradation. To bring these knowledge systems back to use, Laureano listed the following set of principles:

1. Enhancement of local resources;
2. The ability in local management;
3. Low costs that can be spent at a local level;
4. The preference for a high quantity of labour force rather than capital;
5. The close relationship with the environment;
6. Production cycles and consumption that mutually integrate;
7. Propensity towards zero emissions,

Right: Khaju Bridge (*pol-e khajoo*), Isfahan, Iran, *c* 1650
Computational fluid dynamics (CFD) analysis of the Khaju Bridge shows the airflow across the water surface of the river and through the structure. Careful modulation of airflow combined with evaporative cooling procures a comfortable microclimate. (Temporary licences sponsored by EnSight®)

which means that every activity can feed another one;

8. Self-enhancement and autopoiesis (self-regeneration);
9. A multipurpose system and the interrelationship between technological results, cultural and aesthetic values;
10. Accurate resource management;
11. Place and energy saving;
12. Ecosystem management;
13. The integrated project.[73]

Emphasis shifts therefore to the time- and context-specific embeddedness of architectures and their auxiliary relation to multiple local systems.

Today the label 'added value' is frequently used when a project appears to deliver more than has been demanded in the brief. This tendency often leads to the commodification of conditions that may eventually also include auxiliary relations like, for instance, the environmental modulation capacity of the Khaju Bridge and its consequent role as a social space. This may not be the best way forward in that 'added value' will tend to be among the first items to be scrapped when short-term economic interests reign. Instead, principles such as the ones described by Laureano above might need to become mandatory through local planning regulations that are directly informed by context-specific conditions.

The question is who the stakeholders are that might be involved in facilitating the implementation of the complex design required by first-degree auxiliary architectures. How might one convince potential stakeholders to invest in such designs? Or, conversely, how might one convince the policy makers, legislators and regulators that it is necessary to secure the implementation of such traits in the built environment?

At any rate, what can be done at this stage is to develop the approach, produce analyses and reliable data and communicate these to the public, to the policy makers and to the potential stakeholders. This is the mission of the Sustainable Environment Association.

Multiple Grounds and Settlement Patterns

Among the most fundamental causes of *discrete* architectures are the understanding and treatment of the ground as a single level or datum, and the consequences this approach has for urban and architectural design. The ground is typically divided up into parcels that are allocated for use and regulated regarding the maximum allowance of building size in terms of footprint, height and floor area ratio. This has led to the emergence of the now commonplace figure-ground diagram – a two-dimensional solid–void depiction of the city in plan, with buildings shown as black figures or so-called *poché* against the white canvas of the unbuilt open space, which largely evolved from the maps of Rome produced by Leonardo Bufalini and Giambattista Nolli in 1551 and 1748 respectively. Interestingly Nolli depicted the inner spaces of important buildings also in white, thus foregrounding the continuity of publicly accessible space, a characteristic that is missing in later figure-ground maps. These efforts ushered in a still-continuing tradition of surveying and planning of the built environment and reliance on the plan for the study of urban morphology and urban planning and design. This exclusive reliance on the plan and the associated figure-ground approach as the primary devices evidently prevents the design of settlement patterns that cannot be described in plan, in particular extended threshold conditions, extremely dense settlement morphologies and the multiplication of grounds on an architectural and urban scale.

In contrast, architectural history is full of examples of planned and evolving projects that cannot be described in a figure-ground manner. These projects tend to multiply the ground in one way or another. One example is Çatalhöyük, the largest Neolithic settlement yet found. Dating to between c 6,500 and c 5,500 BC, it is located in the Konya plain in Central Anatolia (Turkey). Estimates of its population vary from 5,000 up to 8,000 inhabitants. This density of population brought with it dramatic 'developments in town planning, architecture, agriculture, … technology and religion', as Charles Gates explained.[74] Gates described the settlement as follows:

> The houses clustered together, their walls touching those of their neighbours. Although small courtyards connected by streets lined the edges of the excavated area, within the cluster courts existed but streets did not. People entered houses from the flat rooftops, descending to the floor by means of ladders. Since the town lay on sloping ground, the height of the roofs varied.[75]

This settlement was characterised by a duplication of the datum on which the buildings were erected. On the duplicated raised datum, free movement was facilitated. Thus the provisional datum of the nomadic tradition was re-enabled, yet restrained by the elevated perimeter of the settlement.

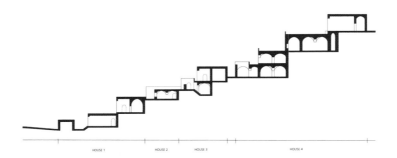

HOUSE 1   HOUSE 2   HOUSE 3   HOUSE 4

HOUSE 1   HOUSE 2

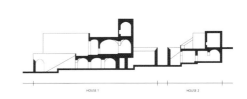

HOUSE 1   HOUSE 2

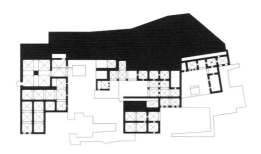

Mardin, Southeast Anatolia, Turkey
The settlement pattern of Mardin is characterised by the utilisation of the steeply sloping terrain in multiplying the ground datum through the use of roof terraces of buildings that double up as front yards and entrance areas for the buildings above (top). The compact sectional and plan arrangement (bottom left) based on adherence to a range of unit sizes and layouts (bottom right) results in an urban fabric that is so dense that it cannot be described by way of figure-ground diagrams. (Drawn after E Füsun Alioğlu, *Mardin – Şehir Dokusu ve Evler*, second edition, Türkiye Ekonomik ve Toplumsal Tarih Vakfı (Istanbul), 2003)

Descending within the cluster from the second datum implied entry into an enclosed space – the interior of the house or, alternatively, a protected court. The dense fabric of the settlement was therefore neither disassociated into discrete figures, nor did it reduce the ground to a singular datum. Instead, a much more intricate relation was established, in which the confined courtyards and the interiors of the houses constitute different degrees of enclosure. Through this sectional articulation, inner perimeters are defined on the duplicated datum wherever roof surfaces are absent. Whatever the historical reasons for the raised datum might have been, it seems useful for a projective outlook to assume an integral reasoning that incorporates social arrangements and spatial formation, and the provisions made by the doubled datum in connection with the pocket-like spaces enfolded within the lower and upper datum.[76]

Another example, the city of Mardin in Turkey, is situated on a south-facing mountain slope that overlooks the southeastern Anatolian plateau and the northern Syrian plains. Mardin is located at an altitude of 1,083 metres, and the Köppen climate classification designates its climate a cold semi-arid. The city is thought to date back to the third century AD, and historically benefited from its strategic location relative to trade routes that tied into the silk routes. It is characterised by its dense terraced fabric of Arabian-style buildings. The design of the introverted mostly two-storey buildings and the very dense and compact settlement adhere to the topography of the steeply sloped hill and to the local climatic conditions. These conditions determined the orientation of the buildings, as well as the density of the built fabric and the more detailed layout of the dwellings, in response to the pronounced difference between hot dry summers and very cold winters of the Anatolian plateau. The narrow inner streets of the city run along the height lines, as well as up- and downhill, catering for the circulation of pedestrians and goods. On numerous occasions buildings bridge over the narrow streets, in particular when intersections are located on private plots. The stepped roof terraces are often part of the circulation and serve in many cases as datum for the set-back building above. The figure-ground arrangement is defied through this doubled datum of the roof terraces, and interestingly there seems to be no conflict arising from the public appropriation of private space for the purpose of circulation. In this way the doubling of the datum facilitates climate- and terrain-specific integration between architectures, circulation and settlement organisation.[77]

Also of interest are the approaches to the design of fortifications that began to evolve in Italy in the 15th century in response to the development of new types of cannons and ammunition. These new star-shaped citadels that protected towns provided better for the cannonry of the defenders, and featured bastions – outward-projecting structures – that served to eliminate blind spots. The citadels sat low in the ground and were surrounded by moats. This feature protected the walls from direct shelling. In the 16th century further features were added. The moats received glacis – artificial slopes that inclined towards the citadel to keep attackers under the line of fire. The military engineer and field marshal Sébastien Le Prestre, Marquis de Vauban (1633–1707) was particularly recognised for his skills in designing such fortifications, improving existing structures in numerous French cities and leading the construction of over 30 new ones including those at Brest, Dunkirk and Freiburg im Breisgau. While these citadels do not multiply the ground per se, they offer another useful feature: the articulation of the ground as provision. Articulation of the ground thus entails particularisation of space.

The citadels' articulation of ground as particularisation of space resonates with David Leatherbarrow's analysis of a specific lineage of modernist work that he traces from Frank Lloyd Wright and Rudolf Schindler to Richard Neutra and that he positions with the following questions:

> Can we … actually envisage an architecture, an enclosure of inhabitable space, without walls, or without very many of them? Can we think of a set of rooms or of a building without an elaborate apparatus of upright space-dividing elements joined together to form corners and therefore enclosures?[78]

Neutra's work points in an interesting direction in that the articulation of the ground or ceiling surface forms a 'structured topography',[79] which in turn articulates a particularised space:

> that includes where I am, which is to say where the things I now need are within reach, a middle distance, and an expansion towards the clear blue horizon: an equipmental, practical, and environmental horizon. Not one can be separated from the others, hence a lateral spread of an ensemble that integrates these 'rings' into one field, terrain or topography – the dining room, the street, and the town or landscape – differentiated but reciprocating.[80]

In his reading of Neutra's work, Leatherbarrow thus emphasised the integration of the multiplications of 'building levels' and their particular articulation. Space is concurrently continuous and locally particularised

Johan Bettum, Michael
Hensel, Nopadol
Limwatankul, Chul Kong,
A Thousand Grounds:
Tectonic Landscape –
Spreebogen, A New
Governmental Center for
Berlin Urban Design Study,
Architectural Association,
London, UK, 1992–3
The folding of landscape and
built mass into a multiple-
ground arrangement was
developed through a series
of conceptual models.

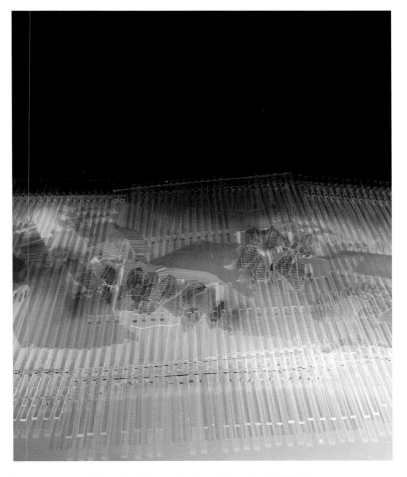

by the topographic articulation of horizontal surface(s). This leaves open
the articulation of enclosure and the articulation of threshold and spatial
transition. As discussed in the preceding sections of this chapter, a singular
and non-spatial enclosure, whether opaque or transparent, eliminates gradual
transition and tends to divide interior from exterior: it renders architectures de
facto discrete. Planar screen walls maintain the connection between exterior
and interior but provide no spatial transition. Spatial screen walls can provide
both. In so doing they support a 'structured topography' of 'differentiated
but reciprocating' horizons.

Johan Bettum, Michael Hensel, Nopadol Limwatankul, Chul Kong, A Thousand Grounds: Tectonic Landscape – Spreebogen, A New Governmental Center for Berlin Urban Design Study, Architectural Association, London, UK, 1992–3
Top: A programme and event map shows the various tectonic and landscape systems that organise the site and its potential for use over time.
Bottom: Axonometric indicating spatial transitions and degrees of interiority in conjunction with landscape surfaces and other spatial elements such as plantation fields and densities.

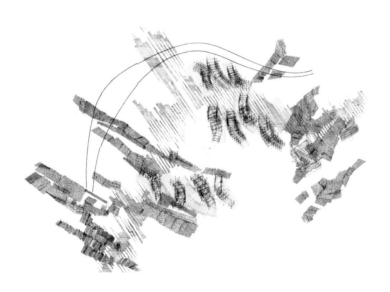

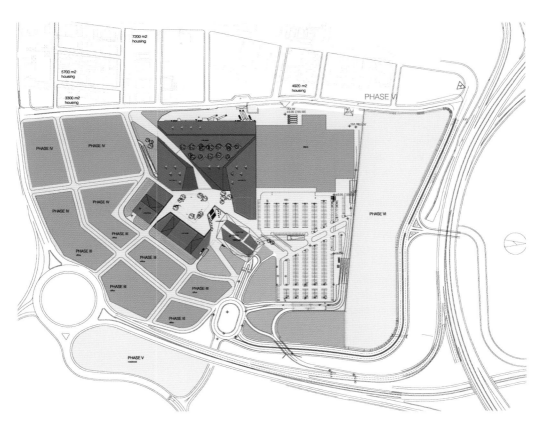

7200 m2
housing

5700 m2
housing

3300 m2
housing

4920 m2
housing

PHASE VI

PHASE IV

PHASE IV

PHASE IV

PHASE III
office

PHASE III
office

PHASE III
office

PHASE III
office

PHASE III
office

PHASE VI

PHASE V
residential

Above and Overleaf:
Foreign Office Architects,
Meydan Retail Complex
and Multiplex, Istanbul,
Turkey, 2007
The section and plan of the
Meydan project show the
multiplication of the ground
datum as landscaped and
publicly accessible surfaces.

Returning to the question of multiple-ground settlements, it is of interest to examine related contemporary approaches. The entry by the Architectural Association Graduate Design Group (AAGDG) for the 'Spreebogen – New Governmental Center for Berlin' competition of 1992–3 aimed at the design of a tectonic landscape consisting of multiple grounds into which the required building volumes were enfolded as a series of nested box-in-box sections with multiple envelopes. The scheme was accompanied by a water-landscape and water-management plan that involved the river Spree and a rotational plantation scheme. However, the scheme failed to develop a corresponding architectural resolution to the design. From 1995 to 1998 OCEAN UK attempted to further articulate this approach on an urban and architectural scale. On an urban scale this involved the development of design guidelines for a 'sectional urbanism':

> Sectional design policies interrelate strata of urban public activity
> surfaces, built volume, interiorised public and private space, and
> urban landscape systems. Sectionally generated space liberates
> mass from static ground.[81]

The enfolding of landscape and built mass into a tectonic
landscape was pursued in a series of unbuilt projects by OCEAN
UK such as the Arabianranta Masterplan (1995–6) and the
Lasipalatsi Media Square (1996), both for Helsinki, and the entry
for the 'Kyoto for the 21st Century' competition (1997).[82]

A number of other projects with similar aims are also
noteworthy. Among these is Foreign Office Architects' Meydan
project in Istanbul (2007) where, not unlike in their Yokohama
International Ferry Terminal project (competition 1994,
completion 2002), a landscaped surface continues onto the built
mass. Moreover, the Meydan project also features screen-type brick walls that
help to modulate the microclimate. While such projects are not yet intensified
multiple-ground schemes, they nevertheless enable the coexistence of
landscape and built mass in the same footprint, and maintain a ground
surface made from soil.

Above: Foreign Office
Architects, Meydan Retail
Complex and Multiplex,
Istanbul, Turkey, 2007
The aerial photograph
shows the Meydan complex
as a continuation of the
landscaped surface of the
wider area.

NEKTON STUDIO's second-prize *Turf City* project for the International
Reykjavik Airport redevelopment competition (2008) delivers an image of an
extensive use of the design approach already present in the Meydan project.
In this scheme each building volume features a landscaped turf roof, often
directly connected with the main ground datum. While this project does
not seek entirely to fuse landscape and built mass, it manages to integrate
different kinds of building morphologies ranging from separate volumes to
an extensive use of the mat-building typology into its expansive multiple-

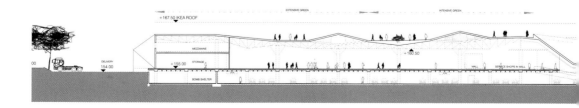

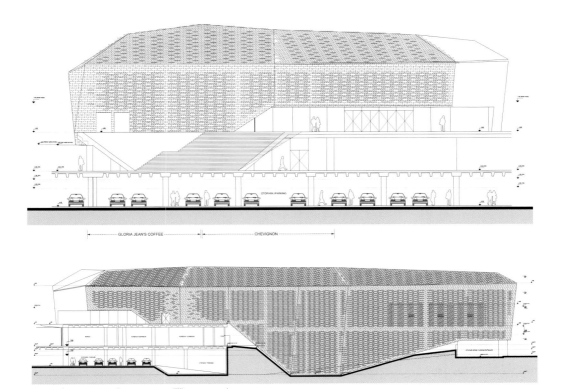

Above: Foreign Office
Architects, Meydan Retail
Complex and Multiplex,
Istanbul, Turkey, 2007
The building envelopes of
the Meydan project consist
of brick screen walls and set-
back climate envelopes.

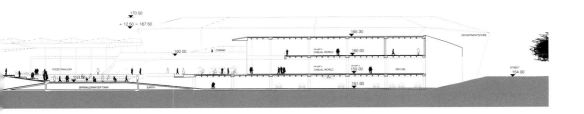

ground scheme.[83] This multiple-ground project is perhaps one of the largest of its kind and the one that came the closest to realisation. It would have been very interesting to see if the Icelandic government would have been prepared to put the necessary policies in place to enable the actualisation of the project's full potential. Surely this project would have had an enormous impact on reconceptualising urban design on many levels and offered an opportunity to develop unprecedented policies based on Urban Ecology research. While urban fabric is commonly characterised by discontinuities due to differentiated land use, large infrastructure, etc, the *Turf City* project could have enabled the coexistence of a continuous natural environment and built environment due to its reliance on sectional and spatial design.

However, more often than not, contemporary multiple-ground projects do not consider context-specific soil composition and associated microclimatic modulation. Soil composition, as well as soil thermal and moisture regimes

Above: NEKTON STUDIO, *Turf City*, Second-Prize Entry in Reykjavik Airport Redevelopment Competition, 2008
The rendered aerial view of the scheme shows the existing ground datum and the second datum that results from the landscaped roofscape of the proposed mix of building typologies.

Opposite: NEKTON STUDIO, *Turf City*, Second-Prize Entry in Reykjavik Airport Redevelopment Competition, 2008
The masterplan shows the proposed mix of block and building typologies and the transitions between them. The extensive use of mat-building typologies makes it possible to articulate a publicly accessible roofscape that doubles the ground.

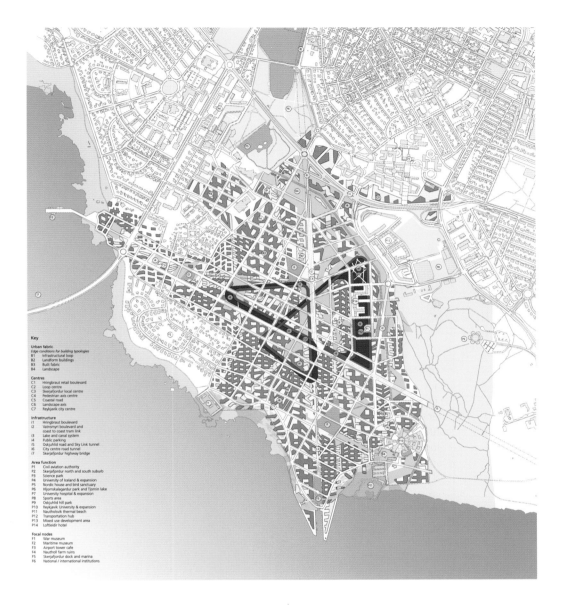

Key

Urban fabric
Edge conditions for building typologies
B1   Infrastructural loop
B2   Landform buildings
B3   Built fabric
B4   Landscape

Centres
C1   Hringbraut retail boulevard
C2   Loop centre
C3   Skerjafjordur local centre
C4   Pedestrian axis centre
C5   Coastal road
C6   Landscape axis
C7   Reykjavik city centre

Infrastructure
i1   Hringbraut boulevard
i2   Vatnsmyri boulevard and
      coast to coast tram link
i3   Lake and canal system
i4   Public parking
i5   Oskjuhlid road and Sky Link tunnel
i6   City centre road tunnel
i7   Skerjafjordur highway bridge

Area function
P1   Civil aviation authority
P2   Skerjafjordur north and south suburb
P3   Science park
P4   University of Iceland & expansion
P5   Nordic house and bird sanctuary
P6   Hljomskalagardur park and Tjornin lake
P7   University hospital & expansion
P8   Sports area
P9   Oskjuhlid hill park
P10   Reykjavik University & expansion
P11   Nautholsvik thermal beach
P12   Transportation hub
P13   Mixed use development area
P14   Loftleidir hotel

Focal nodes
F1   War museum
F2   Maritime museum
F3   Airport tower cafe
F4   Nautholl farm ruins
F5   Skerjafjordur dock and marina
F6   National / international institutions

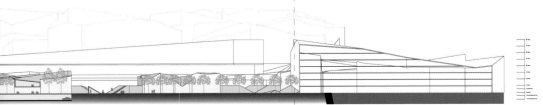

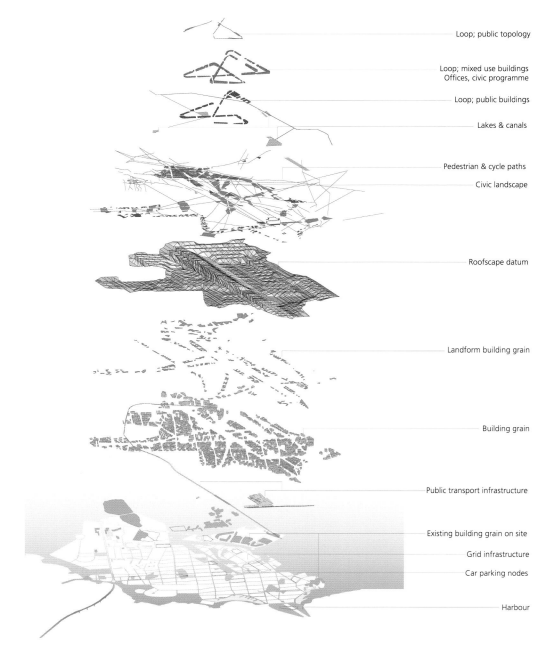

Loop; public topology

Loop; mixed use buildings
Offices, civic programme

Loop; public buildings

Lakes & canals

Pedestrian & cycle paths

Civic landscape

Roofscape datum

Landform building grain

Building grain

Public transport infrastructure

Existing building grain on site

Grid infrastructure

Car parking nodes

Harbour

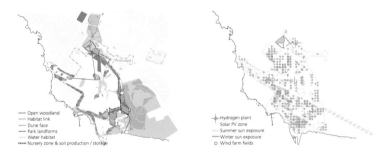

Previous spread below:
NEKTON STUDIO, *Turf City*, Second-Prize Entry in Reykjavik Airport Redevelopment Competition, 2008
Sample section showing the relation between built mass and landscape surface and the doubling of the datum as a publicly accessible landscaped roofscape.

Right: NEKTON STUDIO, *Turf City*, Second-Prize Entry in Reykjavik Airport Redevelopment Competition, 2008
Top: Example of a mat-building typology with a publicly accessible roofscape.
Right: Landscape types.
Far right: Renewable energy scheme.

Opposite: NEKTON STUDIO, *Turf City*, Second-Prize Entry in Reykjavik Airport Redevelopment Competition, 2008
The exploded axonometric shows the different systems that make up the landscaped urban scheme, including built volume, infrastructure and circulation, waterways, landscape and roofscape datum.

are of key importance for the built environment to be in the service of the natural environment. Richard Bardgett and David Wardle pointed out that:

> Traditionally, the aboveground and belowground components of ecosystems have frequently been considered in isolation from one another. However … the last two decades have witnessed a proliferation of studies exploring the influence that these components exert on each other, and the fundamental role that aboveground–belowground interactions play in controlling the structure of terrestrial ecosystems.[84]

Knowledge of the benefits of using soil as a roofing material for vernacular buildings has existed locally throughout history, but its possible climatic and ecological ramifications on a much larger scale remain largely unexplored. It would seem that the notion of the *tectonic landscape* and the potential of *multiple grounds* provide an adequate vehicle for such research precisely because they challenge discrete architecture.

References

1 P Reitan, 'Sustainability Science – And What's Needed Beyond Science', *Sustainability: Science, Practice, & Policy*, Vol 1, No 1, 2005, pp 77–80 (p 77) (online: http://sspp.proquest. com/archives/vol1iss1/ communityessay.reitan.pdf [accessed 10 April 2012]).

2 K Frampton, 'Towards a Critical Regionalism: Six Points for an Architecture of Resistance', in H Foster (ed), *The Anti-Aesthetic: Essays on Postmodern Culture*, Bay Press (Port Townsend, WA), 1983, pp 16–30.

3 S Kwinter, *Architectures of Time: Toward a Theory of the Event in Modernist Culture*, MIT Press (Cambridge, MA), 2001, p 14.

4 B Holmes, 'Earth: The Comeback', *New Scientist*, 3 October 2009, p 32.

5 See: CW Churchman, 'Operations Research as a Profession', *Management Science*, Vol 17, No 2, 1970, pp B37–53; G Midgley, *Systemic Intervention: Philosophy, Methodology and Practice*, Kluwer Academic / Plenum (New York), 2000.

6 W Ulrich, 'Boundary Critique', in HG Daellenbach and RL Flood (eds), *The Informed Student Guide to Management Science*, Thomson (London), 2002, pp 41–2 (p 41).

7 P Martens, 'Sustainability: Science or Fiction?', *Sustainability: Science, Practice, & Policy*, Vol 1, No 2, 2006, pp 36–41 (p 38).

8 WC Clark, 'Sustainability Science: A Room of its Own', *Proceedings of the National Academy of Science*, Vol 104, 2007, pp 1737–8 (online: http://fiesta.bren.ucsb. edu/~gsd/595e/docs/45.%20 Clark_Sustainability_Sci_A_ Room.pdf [accessed 5 December 2011]).

9 See: P Blundell Jones, 'Organic Architecture, Past and Present', in P Van Loocke and Y Joye (eds), *Organic Aesthetics and Generative Methods in Architectural Design: Communication & Cognition*, Vol 36, No 3–4, 2003, pp 137–56.

10 TR Oke, *Boundary Layer Climates*, second edition, Routledge (London), 1987, p 3.

11 Ibid, p 6.

12 Ibid, pp 4–5.

13 NJ Rosenberg, BL Blad and SB Verma, *Microclimate: The Biological Environment*, second edition, John Wiley & Sons (Chichester), 1983, p 1.

14 M Addington, and D Schodek, *Smart Materials and Technologies for the Architecture and Design Professions*, Architectural Press / Elsevier (Oxford), 2005, p 39.

15 JM Dinwoodie, *Timber: Its Nature and Behaviour*, second edition, E & FN Spon (London; New York), 2000, p 49.

16 See: FH Schweingruber, *Wood Structure and Environment*, Springer (Berlin; Heidelberg; New York), 2007; BJ Zobel and JP van Buijtenen, *Wood Variation: Its Causes and Control*, Springer (Berlin; London; New York), 1989.

17 See: A Wagenführ, *Die strukturelle Anisotropie von Holz als Chance für technische Innovationen*, Hirzel / Verlag der Sächsischen Akademie der Wissenschaften zu Leipzig (Leipzig), 2008.

18 See: FL Bunnell and GB Dunsworth, *Forestry and Biodiversity: Learning How To Sustain Biodiversity In Managed Forests*, UBC Press (Vancouver; Toronto), 2009.

19 LT Haugen, *Shaping Wood: The Material is the Mechanism*, masters dissertation, AHO – Oslo School of Architecture and Design (Oslo), 2010.

20 See, for example: J Vincent, *Structural Biomaterials*, revised edition, Princeton University Press (Princeton), 1990; W Nachtigall, *Bionik – Grundlagen und Beispiele für Ingenieure und Naturwissenschaftler*, second edition, Springer (Berlin; London; New York), 2002.

21 R Banham, *The Architecture of the Well-Tempered Environment*, University of Chicago Press (Chicago, IL) / The Architectural Press (London), 1969.

22 R Banham, *The Architecture of the Well-Tempered*

Environment [1969], University of Chicago Press (Chicago, IL), second edition, 1984, p 18.

23 P Sloterdijk, 'Atmospheric Politics', in B Latour and P Weibel (eds), *Making Things Public*, MIT Press (Cambridge, MA; London) / ZKM Centre for Art and Media (Karlsruhe), 2005, pp 944–51 (p 944).

24 Ibid, pp 944–5).

25 Ibid, p 945.

26 See, for example: M Dudek, *Architecture of Schools: The New Learning Environments*, Architectural Press (Oxford), 2000.

27 D Leatherbarrow, 'Architecture's Unscripted Performance', in B Kolarevic and AM Malkawi (eds), *Performative Architecture: Beyond Instrumentality*, Spon Press (New York), 2005, pp 6–19 (p 12).

28 F Nicol and L Pagliano, 'Allowing for Thermal Comfort in Free-Running Buildings in the New European Standard EN 15251', Second PALENC Conference and 28th AIVC Conference on Building Low Energy Cooling and Advanced Ventilation Technologies in the 21st Century, *PALENC*, Vol 2, 2007, pp 708–11 (p 708).

29 Ibid, p 709.

30 Addington and Schodek, *Smart Materials and Technologies for the Architecture and Design Professions*, op cit, p 7.

31 Oke, *Boundary Layer Climates*, op cit, p 33.

32 See: P Atkins, *The Laws of Thermodynamics*, Oxford University Press (Oxford), 2010.

33 H Fathy, *Natural Energy and Vernacular Architecture: Principles and Examples with reference to Hot Arid Climates*, University of Chicago Press (Chicago, IL), 1986.

34 Ibid, pp 48–9.

35 D Leatherbarrow, *Architecture Oriented Otherwise*, Princeton Architectural Press (New York), 2009, p 26.

36 M Hensel and A Menges (eds), *Morpho-Ecologies*, AA Publications (London), 2006; M Hensel and A Menges, *Form Follows Performance – Arch +*, Vol 188, July 2008.

37 Leatherbarrow, 'Architecture's Unscripted Performance', op cit, p 12.

38 S Behling and S Behling, *Solar Power: The Evolution of Sustainable Architecture*, Prestel (Munich; London; New York), 2000, p 120.

39 Leatherbarrow, *Architecture Oriented Otherwise*, op cit.

40 Ibid, p 9.

41 A Colquhoun, 'The Significance of Le Corbusier', *Collected Essays in Architectural Criticism*, Black Dog (London), 2009, pp 193–200 (p 199).

42 Leatherbarrow, *Architecture Oriented Otherwise*, op cit, p 33.

43 Ibid, pp 37–8.

44 Ibid, p 34.

45 F Hoebel, 'The Inseparable Harmony of Within and Without', *Egon Eiermann (1904–1970): Architect and Designer*, Hatje Cantz (Ostfildern-Ruit, Germany), 2004, pp 74–82.

46 Ibid, p 79.

47 E Eiermann, 'Excerpts from an Interview', *Bauwelt*, Vol 64, 1973, p 13.

48 See, for example: M Hensel, D Sunguroğlu Hensel, M Gharleghi and S Craig, 'Towards an Architectural History of Performance: Auxiliarity, Performance and Provision in Historical Persian Architectures', *Iran: Past, Present and Future – AD*, Vol 82, No 3, 2012, pp 26–37.

49 M Hensel and D Sunguroğlu Hensel, 'Extended Thresholds II: The Articulated Envelope', in H Ertas, M Hensel and D Sunguroğlu Hensel (eds), *Turkey: At the Threshold – AD*, Vol 80, No 1, 2010, pp 20–25.

50 A Amirkhani, P Baghaie, AA Taghvaee, MR Pourjafar and M Ansari, 'Isfahan's Dovecotes: Remarkable Edifices of Iranian Vernacular Architecture', *Middle East Technical University – Journal of the Faculty of Architecture*, Vol 26, No 1, 2009, pp 177–86 (online: http://jfa.arch.metu.edu.tr/archive/0258-5316/2009/cilt26/sayi_1/177-186.pdf [accessed 12 September 2011]).

51 Ibid.

52 A Bekleyen 'The Dovecotes of Diyarbakir: The Surviving Examples of a Fading Tradition', *The Journal of Architecture*, Vol 14, No 4, 2009, pp 451–64.
53 V Imamoğlu, M Korumaz and C Imamoğlu, 'A Fantasy in Central Anatolian Architectural Heritage: Dove Cotes and Towers in Kayseri', *Middle East Technical University – Journal of the Faculty of Architecture*, Vol 22, No 2, 2005, pp 79–90 (online: http://jfa.arch.metu.edu.tr/archive/0258-5316/2005/cilt22/sayi_2/79-90.pdf [accessed 12 September 2011]).
54 R Graefe, *Vela Erunt: Die Zeltdächer der römischen Theater und ähnlicher Anlagen*, P von Zabern (Mainz), 1979.
55 G Krause-Valdovinos (ed), *Schattenzelte: Sun and Shade – Toldos, Vela (IL series, Vol 30)*, Institute for Lightweight Structures (Stuttgart), 1984.
56 H Hamann and JL Moro, 'Toldos', in ibid, pp 93–103 (p 94).
57 Ibid, p 94.
58 Ibid, p 95.
59 B Burckhardt, 'Convertible Sun Roofs in Japan', in G Krause-Valdovinos (ed), *Schattenzelte: Sun and Shade – Toldos, Vela*, op cit, pp 104–5 (p 104).
60 F Lang, 'Projects and Ideas', in G Krause-Valdovinos (ed), *Schattenzelte: Sun and Shade – Toldos, Vela*, op cit, pp 124–31.
61 G Krause-Valdovinos (ed), *Schattenzelte: Sun and Shade – Toldos, Vela*, op cit.
62 Oke, *Boundary Layer Climates*, op cit, pp 116–17.
63 Ibid, p 116.
64 Fathy, *Natural Energy and Vernacular Architecture*, op cit, p 5.
65 P Laureano, *The System of Traditional Knowledge in the Mediterranean and its Classification with Reference to different Social Groupings: Report prepared for the Secretariat of the Convention to Combat Desertification*, United Nations Convention to Combat Desertification Conference – Committee on Science and Technology, Recife, 16–18 November 1999, p 4.
66 JM Songel, *A Conversation with Frei Otto*, Princeton Architectural Press (New York), 2010, p 11.
67 D Leatherbarrow, *Architecture Oriented Otherwise* – lecture at the Oslo School of Architecture and Design, 28 April 2011.
68 H Chanson, 'Historical Development of Stepped Cascades for the Dissipation of Hydraulic Energy', *Transactions of the Newcomen Society for the Study of the History of Engineering and Technology*, Vol 71, No 2, 2001, pp 295–318.
69 Hensel, Sunguroğlu Hensel, Gharleghi and Craig, 'Towards an Architectural History of Performance', op cit.
70 Laureano, *The System of Traditional Knowledge in the Mediterranean*, op cit.
71 Ibid, p 8, quoting P Laureano, *Sahara, giardino sconosciuto*, Giunti (Florence), 1988.
72 Laureano, *The System of Traditional Knowledge in the Mediterranean*, op cit, p 9.
73 Ibid, p 21.
74 C Gates, *Ancient Cities: The Archaeology of Urban Life in the Ancient Near East and Egypt, Greece and Rome*, Routledge (London), 2003, p 24.
75 Ibid.
76 M Hensel and D Sunguroğlu Hensel, 'Extended Thresholds I: Nomadism, Settlements and the Defiance of Figure-Ground', in H Ertas, M Hensel and D Sunguroğlu Hensel (eds), *Turkey: At the Threshold – AD*, Vol 80, No 1, 2010, pp 14–17.
77 Ibid.
78 D Leatherbarrow, *Uncommon Ground: Architecture, Technology, and Topography*, MIT Press (Cambridge, MA), 2000, p 28.
79 Ibid, p 66.
80 Ibid.
81 M Hensel and T Verebes, *Urbanisations*, Black Dog (London), 1999, p 34.
82 Ibid.
83 On mat-buildings, see: A Smithson, 'How to Recognize and Read Mat Building', in S Sarkis, P Allard and T Hyde (eds), *Case: Le Corbusier's Venice Hospital and the Mat Building Revival*, Prestel (New York), 2001, pp 90–103.
84 RD Bardgett and DA Wardle, *Aboveground–Belowground Linkages: Biotic Interactions, Ecosystem Processes, and Global Change*, Oxford University Press (Oxford), 2010.

The Road(s) Ahead

Needless to say, there are not yet any projects in existence that demonstrate the integration of the concepts of non-discrete and non-anthropocentric architecture and the various traits of performance-oriented architecture. Many questions remain open at this point. This *Primer* constitutes a mere beginning, albeit one that collects efforts spanning two decades by now. While this initial work represents a particular effort in achieving integration, it does not offset the need to remain critical of key aspects of the approach thus far. It is crucial to remain open to further emerging aspects of importance, while also examining much more closely the interrelation between different combinations of the various specific traits of performance-oriented architecture. Now that the initial contours of an integrated discourse are in place, a lot more specific research and research-by-design efforts need to underpin the further development of this approach. The areas of inquiry that require most attention concern questions of ecology, multi-species integration in architecture and also the field of biosemiotics to address more fully questions of environment and subject relations, in particular when the aim is to provide for multiple species. Each of these areas requires concentrated and sustained research efforts. Equally, attention needs to be placed on the detailed analysis of the built and natural environment and their interaction, as well as the identification and further development of modes of inter- and transdisciplinary knowledge production pertaining to performance-oriented architecture.

Through their interaction with the local physical environment, architectures produce microclimatic conditions, whether intended by the architect or not. At present research aims for either the production of tightly defined ranges or, on a more experimental level, the production of generally unspecified wide ranges of heterogeneous conditions. The former tends to operate on defined anthropocentric standards that are determined statistically or in laboratory experiments, while the latter continues to be undecided as the frame of reference and criteria for evaluation remain unclear. The conceptual difficulty is to define what ranges are advantageous relative to local climate and the project-specific ecological intent in multi-species related provisions. This is not a question of optimisation and standardisation in the common sense. Instead it operates on the foregrounding of dynamics and local differences. Yet, it is not entirely clear how fine a range of local and microclimatic differences should be accounted for, how measurements should be devised that might assist in deciding on the former question, and what the architectural response should be. Depending on geography, orientation and exposure, locations within a short distance of each other can experience considerable differences in temperature, humidity, wind speed and so on. One response would be to decide each case individually. However, this might easily come into conflict with the need for legislation and feasibility.

In more general terms the above brings with it the question of the global and local dialectic. Today it is not unusual to contract an architect who is unfamiliar with local circumstances, and it can often be more financially viable to order specific building elements from a far-away manufacturer that can produce at such low cost as to make transport expenses acceptable. The continued drive towards universal practice combined with a scarcity of both resources and a capacity to document, analyse and adapt design approaches to local circumstances present a considerable obstacle to performance-oriented architecture. It is therefore important to make data about local conditions readily available and to pursue a much greater amount of post-occupation analysis. The question is, though, what kind of data is relevant and for what types of contexts and projects? To undertake such research in a feasible manner it would be necessary to embed it in the educational curricula of schools of architecture. After all, developing more pronounced analytical skills and the necessary knowledge of first principles is of vital importance for the pursuit of performance-oriented architecture.

Tackling the question of the ground and the envelope in relation to performance-oriented architecture is a timely undertaking when so many projects today feature elaborate envelope designs, and when landscape urbanism approaches flourish both in architectural education and practice. As with many other aspects related to performance-oriented architecture, a first necessity is to take stock of such promising developments and projects. This will be the topic of a forthcoming book, prepared by Jeffrey Turko and the author, entitled *Grounds and Envelopes: Reshaping Architecture and the Built Environment*.[1] Understanding the built environment in this way as a vast repository of knowledge is key to the further development of performance-oriented architecture. This also includes revisiting architectural history from a performance perspective, as will be the case in a forthcoming book entitled *The Handbook of Sustainable Traditional Architecture*[2] that will introduce 30 case studies of pre-industrial buildings from different contexts, of which various examples have been discussed in this book.

The systems-related question as to what to include in considerations – the aforementioned boundary problem – needs to be addressed in ways that are accessible to architects. As part of his Systems-Oriented Design approach Dr Birger Sevaldson, Professor for Industrial Design at the Oslo School of Architecture and Design, developed a series of 'visual thinking and visual practice' methods, in particular the development of a form of extensive systems visualisation that he calls *GIGA-map*. Sevaldson describes GIGA-maps as 'rich multi-layered design artefacts that integrate systems thinking with designing as a way of developing and internalizing an understanding of a complex field'.[3] As a tool for visualising complex relations in an extensive manner, GIGA-maps can serve the purpose of redrawing system boundaries in a more detailed and expansive manner, or, likewise, the visualisation of multiple system boundaries in relation to different sets of criteria and/or different stakeholder configurations. In this way visual thinking can yield new skills and sensibilities in working with complex conditions. GIGA-maps can also be of use when exploring different strategies and approaches to integrating the different traits of performance-oriented architecture and help maintain an overview over directly or indirectly affected conditions.

Additional subjects for general research might include:

1 Further integration efforts of the specific traits of performance-oriented architecture towards a non-discrete and non-anthropocentric architecture, through sustained research-by-design experiments and the production of empirical knowledge;

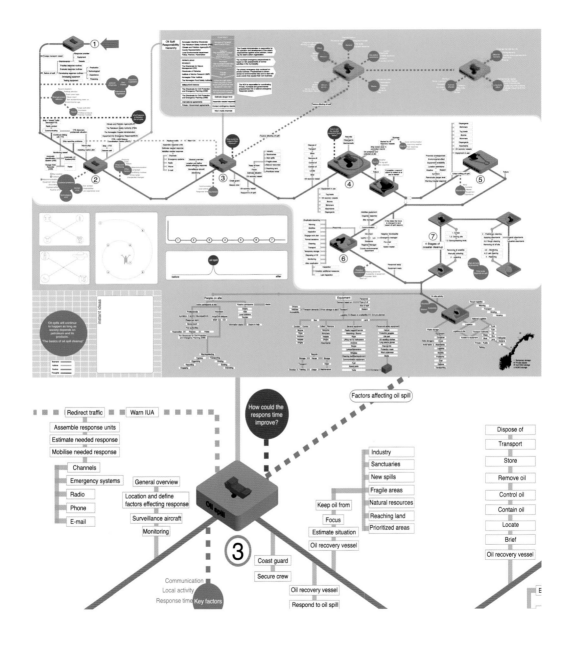

Diploma project by Adrian
Paulsen supervised by
Prof Dr Birger Sevaldson,
'Systems-Oriented Design'
Masters Studio, Oslo
School of Architecture
and Design, 2011
This GIGA-map visualises
the complex web of
actions associated with
oil spill scenarios in the
Oslo Fjord in order to
uncover opportunities
for communication and
procedural improvements
and innovations that can
prevent oil spills instead of
merely reacting to them.

2 Detailed measurements and analysis of the conditions produced by
existing buildings and by design experiments leading to full-scale
construction and description and systematisation of the resulting
microclimatic conditions;

3 Researching the cumulative effects of an increasing number of non-
discrete and non-anthropocentric architectures in one location;

4 Conceptual refinement, restatement or addition to the specific traits of
performance-oriented architecture based on the findings of points 1–3;

5 Development of methods and tools that can assist in working with
complex conditions and dynamics;

6 Close collaboration with ecologists, botanists, zoologists and
microclimatologists towards providing adequate spaces and conditions
for multi-species integration to accomplish a non-anthropocentric
architecture;

7 Close collaboration with biodiversity experts, ecologists, agroecosystems
experts and urban ecologists to ensure that local communities are attuned
to larger system conditions.

It is important, however, that the effort towards developing performance-
oriented architecture does not settle back into a singular hard deterministic
approach, stringent standards and overarching optimisation modes. Instead
it needs to provide problem-specific reliable data and to remain open and
adaptable to changing circumstances so as to be able to be modified in
relation to particular design problems and context-specific conditions.

The difficulties in developing and implementing the further research rest
in the fact that a number of the specific traits of performance-oriented
architecture and the related architectural design approaches are in
contradiction with current policies in numerous countries pertaining to the
built environment and questions of sustainability. Advancing some of the
research in the context of Norway makes the necessary steps somewhat
easier as it is possible to directly interact with policy-making on the
national ministry level. One example, as mentioned before, is the 'Holistic
and Integrated Wood Research' undertaken at the Research Center for
Architecture and Tectonics at the Oslo School of Architecture and Design.

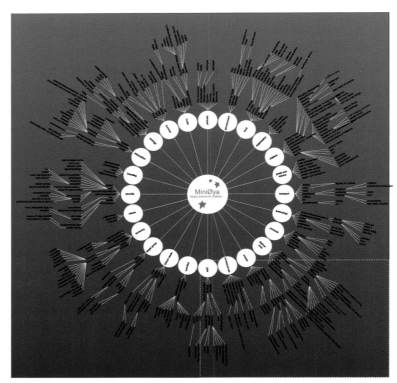

Project by Ingunn
Hesselberg supervised by
Prof Dr Birger Sevaldson,
'Systems-Oriented Design'
Masters Studio, Oslo
School of Architecture
and Design, 2011
In order to outline and
integrate all design,
procedural and managerial
aspects of the proposed
Miniøya Music Festival for
Children, several types of
visualisation techniques are
combined.
Top left: Timeline of the
different activities of the
proposed festival.
Top right: GIGA-map laying
out all effective parameters
in an inclusive manner.
Bottom: The general GIGA-
map is used to explore
three different scenarios of
hierarchy changes between
parameters affecting the
planning process.

This research examines the entire supply and demand chain from forestry to wood-related industries to the construction industry, together with their specific requirements for sustainability. This entails establishing ways of linking biodiversity issues in forestry with an approach to improved wood processing and sorting, and likewise, with the need to arrive at a built environment that is more sustainable based among other aspects on its performative capacity. The Norwegian Ministry of Agriculture and Food, also responsible for forestry, endorses this research and the current Norwegian national government has implemented for the first time guidelines for the development of the built environment in its policy document. This includes a call for more research and for a more advanced use of wood in the built environment. The involvement of numerous stakeholders, including craftsmen, related vocational schools, industries, clients and environmental stakeholders, accompanies this effort. This example also showcases an explicit systems-thinking approach to the specific problem at hand.

A further difficulty that can be anticipated is the need for redefining architectural education to a considerable degree. Greater emphasis needs to be placed on the capacity of students to conduct a clearly identified element of research in their work, as well as to develop to a much greater extent adaptive capacities – that is, the ability to rethink their approach to design whenever necessary – instead of uncritically replicating their familiar approach. Particular efforts in research-by-design have thus far been constrained to masters- and PhD-level studies. Undergraduate studies are typically more exclusively oriented towards teaching the so-called basic knowledge and skills of architects. How these basics are to be defined needs to become a focal point of rethinking architectural education, as fewer and fewer students go on to postgraduate level. If this problem is not tackled, a split in the level of education will occur in which a very large number of professionals may lack the capacity to conduct context-specific research and be unable to adapt their approaches wherever necessary. Likewise, practices that are not versed in conducting the kind of research that may well be expected in the near future will find it difficult to compete for work. An increasing number of recent publications show that more and more practices profile themselves based on their capacity to conduct research. Dr Fredrik Nilsson and the author are currently working on a book that surveys these efforts and portrays the particular approach to research by specific practices of different sizes, from small to medium to large to extra-large. The aim is to deliver a guide for practices that wish to incorporate research more explicitly in their work.

One of the most significant difficulties for the proposed approach is how to convince clients as dominant stakeholders that a long-term and context-specific outlook on architectural design and sustainability is necessary, and that related research will be necessary and needs to be paid for. Even more significantly, they need to be persuaded of the necessity to reduce the total amount of climate-controlled interior relative to the footprint of a building, for the sake of an extended-threshold approach that enables a more heterogeneous space incorporating more exposed areas that can be partially shared with other species. This will require on the one hand the drafting of policies and on the other hand campaigning for the sympathy of clients for such an approach. It could to some extent be accomplished through experimental full-scale constructions that demonstrate the validity and positive effects of such designs. Private and public clients may need to be approached in different ways, also depending on the kind of project that is desired. It would seem that if the development and implementation of related policies is possible, public clients should follow suit in implementing them. As the number of such projects grows, the tolerance and desire of private clients may eventually follow. At any rate it seems evident that long-term sustained research and dissemination efforts must be paralleled with long-term sustained petitioning efforts towards policy makers, public and private clients.

Finally, the continual pursuit of an integrated theoretical framework for performance-oriented architecture necessitates re-questioning almost the entire scope of architectural practice, research and education. While this may be a daunting task, it is nevertheless a worthwhile one. Yet, while performance-oriented architecture might have begun to take shape, its contours are still vague. To move forward will require patience, stamina, resourcefulness and willingness to collaborate in areas of inquiry that are currently well outside the comfort zone of architects. That should constitute an exciting challenge.

References

1 M Hensel and J Turko, *Grounds and Envelopes: Reshaping Architecture and the Built Environment*, Routledge (London), due to be published in 2013.

2 M Hensel, D Sunguroğlu Hensel et al, *The Handbook of Sustainable Traditional Architecture*, John Wiley & Sons (Chichester), 2013.

3 B Sevaldson, 'GIGA-Mapping: Visualisation for Complexity and Systems Thinking in Design', Nordic Design Research Conferences (Helsinki), 2011 (online: http://ocs.sfu.ca/nordes/index.php/nordes/2011/paper/view/409/256 [accessed 2 October 2011]), p 18.

Select Bibliography

Alexander, C, *Notes on the Synthesis of Form*, Harvard University Press (Cambridge, MA), 1964

Behling, S and Behling, S, *Solar Power: The Evolution of Sustainable Architecture*, Prestel (Munich; London; New York), 2000

Eco, U, *The Open Work*, Harvard University Press (Cambridge, MA), 1989; originally published as Eco, U, *Opera Aperta*, Gruppo Editoriale Fabbri, Bompiani, Sonzogno, Etas (Milan), 1962

Fathy, H, *Natural Energy and Vernacular Architecture: Principles and Examples with Reference to Hot Arid Climates*, University of Chicago Press (Chicago, IL), 1986

Grobman, Y and Neuman, E (eds), *Performalism: Form and Performance in Digital Architecture*, Routledge (London), 2012

Harper, JL and Hawksworth, DL, *Biodiversity: Measurement and Estimation*, Chapman & Hall (Oxford), 1995

Hensel, M (ed), *Design Innovation for the Built Environment: Research by Design and the Renovation of Practice*, Routledge (London), 2012

Hensel, M, Hight, H and Menges, A (eds), *Space Reader: Heterogeneous Space in Architecture*, John Wiley & Sons (Chichester), 2009

Hensel, M and Menges, A (eds), *Morpho-Ecologies*, AA Publications (London), 2006

Hensel, M and Sunguroğlu Hensel, D, 'Extended Thresholds I: Nomadism, Settlements and the Defiance of Figure-Ground', in H Ertas, M Hensel and D Sunguroğlu Hensel (eds), *Turkey: At the Threshold – AD*, Vol 80, No 1, 2010, pp 14–17

Hensel, M and Sunguroğlu Hensel, D, 'Extended Thresholds II: The Articulated Envelope', in H Ertas, M Hensel and D Sunguroğlu Hensel (eds), *Turkey: At the Threshold – AD*, Vol 80, No 1, 2010, pp 20–25

Hensel, M and Sunguroğlu Hensel, D, 'Extended Thresholds III: Auxiliary Architectures', in H Ertas, M Hensel and D Sunguroğlu Hensel (eds), *Turkey: At the Threshold – AD*, Vol 80, No 1, 2010, pp 76–83

Hensel, M, Sunguroğlu Hensel, D, Gharleghi, M and Craig, S, 'Towards an Architectural History of Performance: Auxiliarity, Performance and Provision in Historical Persian Architectures', *Iran: Past, Present and Future – AD*, Vol 82, No 3, 2012, pp 26–37

Hensel, M and Turko, J, *Grounds and Envelopes: Reshaping Architecture and the Built Environment*, Routledge (London), 2013

Kolarevic, B and Malkawi, A, *Performative Architecture: Beyond Instrumentality*, Spon (New York), 2005

Kuma, K, *Anti-Object: The Dissolution and Disintegration of Architecture*, AA Publications (London), 2008

Kwinter, S, *Architectures of Time: Toward a Theory of the Event in Modernist Culture*, MIT Press (Cambridge, MA), 2001

Latour, B, *Reassembling the Social: An Introduction to Actor-Network-Theory*, Oxford University Press (Oxford), 2005

Leatherbarrow, D, *Architecture Oriented Otherwise*, Princeton Architectural Press (New York), 2009

Leatherbarrow, D, 'Architecture's Unscripted Performance', in B Kolarevic and AM Malkawi (eds), *Performative Architecture: Beyond Instrumentality*, Spon Press (New York), 2005, pp 6–19

Leatherbarrow, D, *Uncommon Ground: Architecture, Technology, and*

Topography, MIT Press (Cambridge, MA), 2000

Loreau, M, Naeem, S and Inchausti, P, *Biodiversity and Ecosystem Functioning: Synthesis and Perspectives*, Oxford University Press (Oxford), 2002

Marzluff, JM, Shulenberger, E, Endlicher, W, Alberti, M, Bradley, G, Ryan, C, Simon, U and ZumBrunnen, C, *Urban Ecology: An International Perspective on the Interaction between Humans and Nature*, Springer (New York), 2008

Oke, TR, *Boundary Layer Climates*, second edition, Routledge (London), 1987

Reichholf, JH, *Stabile Ungleichgewichte – Die Ökologie der Zukunft*, Suhrkamp (Frankfurt), 2008

Reitan, P, 'Sustainability Science – And What's Needed Beyond Science', *Sustainability: Science, Practice, & Policy*, Vol 1, No 1, 2005, pp 77–80 (online: http://sspp.proquest.com/archives/vol1iss1/communityessay.reitan.pdf [accessed 10 April 2012])

Rosenberg, NJ, Blad, BL and Verma, SB, *Microclimate: The Biological*

Environment, second edition, John Wiley & Sons (Chichester), 1983

Sevaldson, B, 'GIGA-Mapping: Visualisation for Complexity and Systems Thinking in Design', Nordic Design Research Conferences (Helsinki), 2011 (online: http://ocs.sfu.ca/nordes/index.php/nordes/2011/paper/view/409/256 [accessed 2 October 2011])

Ulrich, W, 'Boundary Critique', in HG Daellenbach and RL Flood (eds), *The Informed Student Guide to Management Science*, Thomson (London), 2002, pp 41–2

Vandermeer, J, van Noordwijk, M, Anderson, J, Ong, C and Perfecto, I, 'Global Change and Multi-Species Agroecosystems: Concepts and Issues', *Agricultures, Ecosystems and Environment*, Vol 67, 1998, pp 1–22

Progressive Architecture, *Performance Design* issue, August 1967

Report of the World Commission on Environment and Development: Our Common Future, 1987, transmitted to the General Assembly as an Annex to *Document A/42/427 – Development and International Co-operation: Environment*, Chapter 6: 'Species and Ecosystems: Resources for Development' (online: http://www.un-documents.net/ocf-06.htm#I [accessed 3 December 2011])

Index

Picture Credits

The author and the publisher gratefully acknowledge the people who gave their permission to reproduce material in this book. While every effort has been made to contact copyright holders for their permission to reprint material, the publishers would be grateful to hear from any copyright holder who is not acknowledged here and will undertake to rectify any errors or omissions in future editions.

l = left, r = right, t = top, b = bottom

Cover image © Michael Hensel. With thanks to: Julia King and Louis Gadd (layer 1); Dae Song Lee (layer 2).

pp 35, 36, 37 © R&Sie(n); pp 38, 39 © Steven Holl Architects; pp 56, 59, 80 © Michael Hensel; p 100 Photography © Michael Hensel and Defne Sunguroğlu Hensel; p 69 Photography © Defne Sunguroğlu Hensel, 2009; pp 78, 79 Photography © Defne Sunguroğlu Hensel; p 93 © Defne Sunguroğlu Hensel / SEA – Sustainable Environment Association; pp 62, 63, 64 Courtesy Linn Tale Haugen (Diploma Project AHO), © Oslo School of Architecture and Design, Norway, 2010; pp 66, 67, 68 Courtesy Wing Yi Hui and Lap Ming Wong (Responsive Wood Architectures Studio Project), © Oslo School of Architecture and Design, Norway, 2010; p 75 © Iconotec; p 77 Courtesy Joseph Kellner and David Newton (Proto-Architectures Studio), © Rice School of Architecture, Houston, Texas, 2004; pp 81, 82 © Cloud 9; pp 83, 84 © studioINTEGRATE; pp 86, 87, 88 Courtesy Nasrin Kalbasi and Dimitrios Tsigos (Copenhagen Playhouse Competition Entry, Diploma Unit 4), © Architectural Association, London, UK, 2001; pp 89, 90 Courtesy Hani Fallaha and Dimitrios Tsigos (Experimental House, Diploma Unit 4), © Architectural Association, London, UK, 2002–3; p 91 ©OCEAN Design Research Association; p 92 Courtesy Joakim Hoen (Diploma Project), © Oslo School of Architecture and Design, Norway, 2011; pp 111, 112 Joakim Hoen and Rikard Jaucis (Auxiliary Architectures Studio) © Oslo School of Architecture and Design, 2010; pp 94 114, 115 © Salmaan Craig, Mehran Gharleghi, Michael Hensel, Amin Sadeghy, and Defne Sunguroğlu Hensel - SEA – Sustainable Environment Association; pp 97, 98, 99 Courtesy Kazutaka Fujii (Micro-Ecologies Studio), © London Metropolitan University, UK, 2006–7; pp 102, 103 Photography © Melih Uçar; pp 104, 105, 106, 109, 110 ©OCEAN Design Research Association; pp 107, 108 Las Piedras del Cielo – Membrane Shelter – Open City Ritoque, Scarcity and Creativity in Latitude 33 Master-Studio, © Oslo School of Architecture and Design, Norway, 2012; p 118 Drawn after Füsun Alioğlu, E. (2003). Mardin – Şehir Dokusu ve Evler. 2nd Edition. Istanbul: Türkiye Ekonomik ve Toplumsal Tarih Vakfı Yayınıdır; p 121 Photography © Nopadol Limwatanakul; p 122 Courtesy Johan Bettum, Michael Hensel, Nopadol Limwatankul, Chul Kong, A Thousand Grounds: Tectonic Landscape – Spreebogen, A New Governmental Center for Berlin Urban Design Study, © Architectural Association, London, UK, 1992–3; pp 123, 124-5, 125 © Foreign Office Architects; p 124 (t) © Foreign Office Architects/ Photography: Courtesy Metro Management; pp 126, 126-7, 127, 128, 129 © Jeffrey P. Turko & Gudjon T. Erlendsson/ NEKTON STUDIO; p 136 Diploma project by Adrian Paulsen supervised by Prof Dr Birger Sevaldson, 'Systems-Oriented Design' Masters Studio, © Oslo School of Architecture and Design, 2011; p 138 Project by Ingunn Hesselberg supervised by Prof Dr Birger Sevaldson, 'Systems-Oriented Design' Masters Studio, © Oslo School of Architecture and Design, 2011.